"I've worked with funeral directors who had to deal with families of presidents and movie stars. They all had a chance at life that most of us will never experience. But what we do have is so much more."

As more and more Americans reconsider what it means to die, texts like this book become an important part of the death-planning process as well as the death-positive movements currently reshaping society's conversations about death. In the family-first spirit of funeral industry writers like Caitlin Doughty, this book guides readers through not only coping with their own loved ones' deaths but also the importance of proper planning. It also enlightens readers on how America's funeral industry standard, with its one-size-fits-all approach to everything from casket size to ceremony expectations, often excludes other cultures and their death practices. It poses how the industry might become more inclusive. Despite the morbid stereotypes readers might apply to a text about the funeral industry, at its core, this book is a celebration of life and a life well-lived, particularly in the service to others during their time of greatest need.

book review by Nicole Yurcaba
-US Review of Books

"What if you knew the day of your impending death, what would you do?" So begins Terrence White's memoir, a slim tome that recounts White's 27 years in the "death-care industry" and offers readers advice regarding planning for death's inevitability and living meaningful lives.

Based on his experiences, White advises readers to protect loved ones by pre-planning and paying for their own funerals. He believes that cremation is "disrespectful" and offers advice to funeral officiants. He also liberally dispenses life-enhancing suggestions, all variations on a central theme: Listen, connect with others, let go, and obey the Golden Rule.

The author writes in a relatable manner, tempering his topic with humor. Amusing anecdotes of funeral planning gone wrong and unusual postmortem desires— "put popcorn in my pockets then cremate me" — provide levity.

Despite the book's flaws, White's unique insight is likely to encourage readers to consider their inescapable demise more carefully, make lifestyle changes while they can, and plan for an event they might prefer to dismiss.

-BlueInk Review

Rest Easy *reconsiders funerals as events that are not dreary, but that instead are a source of strength for the living.*

Terrence White's career memoir *Rest Easy* goes behind the scenes in its coverage of the funeral industry.

Conversational and light, the book moves from observations, as of people at funerals talking about how they really should talk more often, toward approachable recommendations, as with a funny list of fourteen ways to keep in touch that includes telepathy and smoke signals.. Its topical chapters cover everything from funeral planning to the importance of celebrants making personal connections with the families of those who are lost, and its warmhearted narration ably conveys care and concern for others, and its consideration of death as an opportunity for hope and connection is refreshing.

The book progresses from White's first experiences with death and the funeral industry toward his eventual calling to ministry. Still, it is rambling in tone and form: it jumps from a discussion of White's chest pains and family struggles to talking about funeral costs and caring for the homeless. Though its anecdotes are colorful, even sometimes funny, their loose inclusion means that important ideas and specific recommendations are often buried.

Through musing memories of a career in the funeral industry, *Rest Easy* is a memoir that reconsiders funerals as events that are not dreary, but that instead are a source of strength for the living.

JEREMIAH ROOD (November 20, 2020)
-Foreword Review

REST EASY

Rest Easy

A Life's Journey to The Last day

Terrence White

InfusedMedia Co. LLC
www.infusedmedia.co
1-888-251-6088

CONTENTS

Chapter 1

What If

In all the circles of my life, there is one question that seems to get asked by friends or relatives. It is one that will challenge your thoughts.

What if you knew the date and time of your impending death, what would you do? Would you go on a drunken binge? Would you tell all your enemies how you feel? Would you confront your secret flame? Would you max out all your credit cards? How would you organize your every move? Would you tell anyone, or would you keep it to yourself?

There's a million questions that would occupy your thinking. But it is an important, and intriguing scenario, if you were offered the opportunity. Let's face it, that day will come sooner or later. You can postpone it with medicine or good living, but it will come.

We have become very good at preparing for other events, like vacations and weddings. Let's not forget that first house or the arrival of that bundle of joy. We have a timeline in place and a plan for that special day. We involve others and give each of them special instructions. Steve, you bring the ice; Cindy, you bring the flowers; Doug, you bring your wife. We are very good at organizing things like these, and if we're not, we hire someone who is. Let's think along these lines and plan for that last day, as if we know when that is.

I think about my last day and my journey through life. Over the years, there have been ups and downs. There were heartaches, and my heart filled with good moments. I loved some and despised others. But it seems that I fear that I may have done harm where I've traveled, and sometimes it scares me to think about the mistakes I've made, the people I've hurt, the trail I have left for others to follow or trip over. And then I wonder if I'm putting myself on too high of a pedestal for thinking that I may have left that much of an effect on anyone. Yes, others have left a lasting effect on me over the years. But how can I imagine that I have done the same on any level. Chances are, we have all made a lasting effect on the ones we love, on the ones who have loved us, and in some cases, on those whom we may have forgotten.

The idea that we would be faced with a definite deadline, a calendar to prepare for that final moment, would frighten anyone. But it would give you the opportunity to think about your life in CliffsNotes.

I would first try to refer to my past. Like most, I would want to make things right where I have errored. Given the chance, I would think that I would scramble through years of all the bad things I thought I did and try to correct them. Truth is, I, like most, think there's plenty of time. Why not take this time to right all my wrongs?

Alcoholics Anonymous has a formula for this in their twelve-step program. The ninth step suggests to "make direct amends whenever possible, except when to do so would injure them or others."

You would be surprised at the idea that you are the only one worried about your past. Although there could be some relationships that need to be mended, most everyone is more into your present.

What you did in the past has no effect on who you are today unless you allowed that to happen. What is important is how you make others feel now. Are you at peace? Are you always angry? Do you show up late? Do you pay less attention to some who want more?

Pay attention to how others act around you. Do they move away to another part of the room? Or do they smile and greet you with joy?

What if this is your last day, you have twenty-four hours until the moment of your last breath? You are still you.

I would like to think that I would be surrounded by the people who love me and care for me.

> I wish everyone could wake up with a birdie on your shoulder, reminding them that this could be your last day. As you get older, you see how rapidly the years and decades fly by, so I would encourage anyone, no matter the age, to seize their life and be fully present. Savor every moment and go after your dreams. Be relentless in pursuing your happiness. (Theo Rossi)

Most of us live in fear—fear of job loss; fear of economic disparity, of being accepted, of faltering health; and fear of losing a loved one. It seems natural to protect yourself from the elements of those things that are inevitable, such as "end of life." We are constantly looking for ways to extend the number of days left on earth, but seem to ignore ideas to improve each day that we have left. It's simple, really. Find that place in your heart that forgives, loves, and accepts whoever is in front of you. Anger, jealousy, and a lowered disposition has no room in your life anymore. Remember, your life is about to come to a close. You have no time for bad blood. It's time to repair the damage done and move toward that last day carrying a lighter bag.

Follow these nine steps. You have nothing to lose and a lot of love to gain.

1. Accept others even if you get rejected.
2. Walk more. Drive less.
3. Make amends, but don't beg.
4. Surround yourself with the people who love you.
5. Look for ways to improve your days, like meditation.
6. Treat others with respect.
7. Steer clear of people and things that make you angry.
8. Give freely of yourself.
9. Remember that things have no value when you are gone.

I remember a spring day in 1987 when my dad called, asking if he could meet me for lunch the next day. This was a very unusual request from him. Of course, I accepted the invitation, as my curiosity was getting the best of me.

Dad wasn't the kind of guy who would ever interrupt your day, so when he did, it was important.

My relationship with Dad was pretty strong. I loved him and respected him.

He was a very strong-willed man—ex-military, handyman, a man's man, if you will. His humor was sometimes a little off-color, but he was never one to shy away from a good or bad joke.

My mother had passed away early in life. That was 1970. She was a young fifty-year-old. I was seventeen years old and had four siblings to keep me company. (I will talk about this in another chapter.) But Dad seemed lost. Watching him struggle with the loss of his life partner was painful. I watched him grow into a different person for a while. He would be influenced by the wrong people from time to time. It was like watching a teenager grow up. Sometimes you had to step in and guide them in a different direction. Fortunately, Dad respected his kid's opinions at times and would, eventually, curb his flow toward undesirable influences.

Over the years, he met some great people and even married one.

They stayed together for a while, but that didn't last, and he would be all alone once again. I would start to see Dad at my house hanging out with my wife Mary and my daughter Sarah. Sarah was just a baby, but a very active one and smart. She loved seeing Papa. Sarah and Dad would have conversations as if she was all grown up. It all made my day when I would walk in from work and see him sitting in the dining room with Sarah on his knee and my wife Mary across the table smiling at something he just said.

So I was to meet Dad at one of our favorite restaurants in Davenport, Iowa, at a place called the Tick Tock.

We arrived at the same time. As I looked over at him walking toward me, I sensed that this was not going to be a happy occasion. He looked pale, and his eyes seemed dark. As we walked in, he seemed out of breath so we commandeered the closest table to us just to get him a seat.

As we visited, at first, he would ask me questions like, what are my future plans, and do I ever think about going back to school? So I would give a generic response like "I am constantly thinking of my future and a possible return to school." I could tell by his expressions that this was not what this meeting was really about. After a moment of uncomfortable silence, Dad looked at me and said, "I have something I need to tell you, and I don't want you to get upset." I said, "What is it, Dad? You can tell me anything." He started to tell me about a recent diagnosis of an enlarged heart and that the medicine is not doing what they had hoped. He explained to me that he has very little time left on this earth and that he needs to sit with each of his kids to say his last goodbye. My heart reached into my throat and started to choke me. I did not want to cry here in front of him. I held back the tears as long as I could. I wanted to reach over the table and give him a hug, but I knew that if I did, I would break down.

I don't remember what was said after that. I don't even remember what we ate. I just remember how I felt. It was a pain so great that I felt numb and completely oblivious of anything or anybody around me. I remember sitting in my car in that parking lot, watching Dad drive off. I was lost and frightened at the same time. Nothing seemed important anymore. I remember going through a variety of emotions as I sat there. I don't even remember leaving that parking lot or if I finished my day of work. I just remember that pain.

I would call him every day and check on him as he made his rounds to see all of my four siblings. There was no easy way to contact him other than his house phone. After all, it was 1987, and cell phones were not a thing yet.

On the fifth day, I received a call from my oldest brother Jim. Dad was to meet Jim that day and never showed up. I lived closest to Dad so I told Jim that I would drive over to his house to see if he's all right.

Dad lived about fifteen miles from my house, but it seemed like one thousand miles this time.

As I pulled into the driveway, I noticed there were two newspapers still on his front stoop. My biggest fear was seeing any evidence of his demise. And there it was. I stared at the newspapers for a few minutes before I exited my car. It was late in the day, turning dark. Dad never let a day go by without his morning coffee and his newspaper. I had a key to his house since I was the closest relative. My hand shook as I put the key into the door lock. When I opened the door, I could see down the hall and into his living room.

I froze in place as I could see, in the distance, a relaxed man, stretched out on his recliner, TV remote still in hand. While the TV was loud enough for neighbors to hear, there was no other soul around. His can of Diet Pepsi sat on the table next him. He loved Diet Pepsi. As I walked closer, I could tell that my dear old father had no life left.

He was stiff, but peaceful. He warned me that this day would be here soon. I guess that it didn't register that it would be this soon. I stood there looking at a man I always thought would be around, never realizing that time will be our only friend if we just treated it well. Did I say "I love you" enough? Did I show my appreciation for all his guidance through life? Did I make him proud? And then it hit me. There will be no more dad jokes. Those moments of seeing him play with my daughter will be no more. I will never have a chance to see him smile and laugh again.

With tears in my eyes, I reached over and picked up his phone. I called my brother Jim and broke down, bawling like a baby. As I administered the bad news over the phone, I could feel a sense of warmth come over me. It was like something is guiding me through all this, and within no time at all, I was surrounded by the comfort of my brother Jim and a dear friend and priest, Father Jack. Jim lives a good one and a half hours from Dad's place. But it seemed he was teleported just for me. Father Jack and friends from the local funeral home took over as Jim and I stood by. We were together as a family as we watched our dear old dad get loaded into the transport vehicle from the funeral home.

Dad had a timeline. He knew that his days were coming to a close very soon. He opted to use his time to say goodbye to his children.

There never seems to be a good time to say goodbye. You think you have time to mill it over and maybe doctor it up some, just to soften the blow. Truth is, you will never have enough time to soften the blow.

His funeral was a gathering of people whom I haven't seen in years. There were those who appeared out of curiosity and some for a need for their own comfort. There were moments of tears and gracious greetings from family and friends. It was a love fest of sorts. Some loved him for his kindness, some for his money, and then there were some who never thought they would have to say goodbye so soon. To some, he was Jack (a nickname given to him as a young child); to some he was John; but to myself and my siblings, he was Dad.

As I peered into the casket for the first time, I was expecting to see the guy who would grab the garden hose and give me a surprise dowsing on a hot summer day. I wanted to see the man that was there for me when I needed a shoulder to cry on, the guy whom everyone wanted to hang out with at my wedding.

But what I saw was just a body that used to have a soul, a body that was more of a thing than a man. I suppose it looked a little like Dad, but there was no connection to the life that we were celebrating.

There was chatter in the background. I heard a lady tell my sister how special her dad was to her. I looked at the body and imagined Dad piping up and yelling across the room at her. But the body just lay there. No movement, no expression, just a body, a thing. This was not Dad. Dad had left the day he died. This is just a thing, a representation of that dear man. Like a statue or a bust.

I wanted that time back so I could put my arm around the old man and let him know how much he meant to me. I know he would like that.

Drawn by Jim White

This was a true lesson for me. I want to enjoy every day with those I love as often as I can. What this day proved to me is that moment that the last breath is exhaled, that is the end of everything. Sure, life goes on for those left behind, but it goes on without you. I needed to get to work on loving and spend less time on worrying and fighting. I looked at a room full of people who came to give their condolences. I looked over at my sister and brothers. I wanted our family back, but that wasn't going to happen.

Dad knew that his last day was near. He took what time he had left to say goodbye to the people that mattered to him and who loved him back.

I've had the pleasure of ministering eulogies for some who were still breathing as I prepared their send-off. Those were moments of importance for me because I never got to do that for Dad. There's something magical about sitting with a friend and letting them talk about their life story. It's a gift if you can get it. I highly encourage everyone to take some time and learn all you can about the people you love. You will not be disappointed. Sometimes we let our own lives get in the way of knowing how to love others. You can't love them all the way until you really get to know them.

I took for granted a life that I knew, a life that garnered protection for myself and others. One day, I would see the light. I would know the true meaning of love. My only hope is that the world can connect to each other in that light. Free up your spirit to let the life of someone you love in.

Have you noticed that we tend to be drawn to talk shows? We like the interviews. We want to know more about our favorite celebrity. That seems like a fun way to get to know more about someone. Set up an interview. Have a little fun with it. Sometimes a little "outside the box" works.

Remember that someone in your circle may be holding the key to the universe. Stay close. Let them know you care. Ask questions and never be afraid of the answers you get.

I have a friend who loves to travel. He has been all over the world. He has seen things that I can only imagine. I love to listen to him talk about his journeys. More importantly, I enjoy seeing the sparkle in his eyes as he describes a trip into another world.

Just imagine the stories that your grandparents can tell. Let them take you back to a time before you were born. You will be amazed at the gleam in their eyes and the world they can bring alive to you.

I remember being interviewed by a high schooler a few years back. She was given an assignment to interview an older person sixty plus. Her questions were already laid out for her. All she had to do was ask and write down my responses.

One of the questions was, Where was I, and what do I remember about the JFK assassination?

I was sitting in my fifth-grade classroom at Wilson Elementary School in Davenport, Iowa. It was a damp and chilly November day in 1963. Our teacher was called out to the hallway by one of the office people. When she entered back to the classroom, she had tears in her eyes as she walked over to her desk. Her name was Ms. English. She was a strong-willed lady and very direct when she spoke. This time, however, she seemed to lack that self-control that she always carried this time. The class was very quiet, which was very unusual since she always encouraged interaction. But there was a sense of despair that seemed to enter our hearts as we focused on our leader.

As she gathered her composure, she spoke with a crack in her voice and said, "I have some very bad news to tell you all. President Kennedy is dead."

I do not remember what she said next. But I do remember how I felt. There was nothing that could grasp my attention after that moment. Sure, I was only like eleven and not too up on the daily news; but back then, everyone knew who President Kennedy was. We were taught to understand who our elected officials were in those days. Our parents made sure of that.

Well, school let out early, and I and my sister, Sue, who was in the third grade, walked home. There was no conversation between us. All I could think of was being home with Mom and Dad and letting them try to make sense out of all this.

For the next few days, we sat around the old black-and-white screen TV with only three channels. CBS was my dad's favorite because that was the one with Walter Cronkite. Cronkite was the best straight man for news. You never knew what side of the aisle he sat on politically.

We watched as Jack Ruby shot Lee Harvey Oswald live. We watched a horse-drawn caisson carry the casket with our president down Pennsylvania Avenue, also live.

Not once did anyone ask us how we felt about all this. I remember going through a number of thoughts and feelings about the whole assassination experience. I was eleven. I had never been through a death of any kind. I was scared and confused. Was this the new normal? Are people not as good as I have been led to believe? Why would anyone want to shoot this nice man? And then things got really strange. Conspiracy theories were thrown around the house like insults at a Dean Martin roast.

Some of the more colorful theories were as follows:

- Jack Ruby had JFK killed because he and his wife were having an affair.
- Johnson had him killed so he could be president.
- Jackie had him killed because she found out about Marilyn Monroe.
- The mob had him killed because brother Bobby kept investigating them.
- Castro had him killed because of the Bay of Pigs.
- And the best one, Lee Harvey Oswald was having an affair with Jackie.

It just started getting to the point where I stopped listening because I just knew that my teacher would have all the answers when I returned to school.

Anyway, this poor high school girl had to sit and listen to me go on and on about all that. She would look at me with those "when are you going to stop talking" looks every now and then, but she was polite and let me ramble on. When we finished, she thanked me, put her coat on, and headed out the door like she was late for prom.

I never asked her how that assignment worked out. I guess I was afraid of the answer, but many years later, she did tell me that her report was the best in the class. She said her teacher assumed that she asked a lot of questions. Little did she know that her interview subject just never stopped talking.

Now, getting back on track, what would you do if you were messaged with a note that read, "Your last day is tomorrow"?

I've listened to numerous religious leaders telling me and everyone else to prepare yourself for the coming of the Lord. I have always been told that the coming of the Lord meant that was your last day on earth and that could be any day, without warning. And I've listened to TV preachers brag about how they have talked with God and God told them this or that.

I have been disappointed in some religious leaders and their unguided lack of reality to the heavens.

My wife's mother suffered some debilitations to her health in her late years. When she was on her deathbed, she wanted to have a priest come by and administer her last rites. Because she had been in poor shape for such a long time, she had not been inside a church for some years. Mary and I called around to nearby Catholic parishes and was only able to talk with admin folks. In every case, we were told that unless she was a member of their parish, Father would not be available without a nominal fee. Mary and her brother, Chuck, made the decision to pay the fee. The church that she was a member of was no longer in service so we had to act fast. Thank goodness he wore his collar so that she would know that her wishes were honored. He administered the last rites, and you could see a calmness come over my sweet mother-in-law. She lived a few weeks after that, and my Mary and her brother would take turns staying by her side. No one is sure why or even how she hung on as long as she did but I have my theory. I believe that this was her spirit's way of allowing her and her immediate family, Mary and brother Chuck, to spend time together and remember her journey through life. She was an amazing person. Full of love and could make you smile just to see her grin. When she finally passed, we knew that she was at peace. I often think about how wonderful it would have been if I could have delivered her eulogy.

I have read stories about people who have had premonitions or knowing that *the* moment is near for them or a loved one.

Sometimes I wished we all did know of the time and day. I think most of us would act better and show a little more respect for others.

Interestingly enough, after asking this, I looked up some responses on Google, and this is what I found:

- I would use my hand to brush my teeth instead of a hand brush. It has been a long time since I got time to experience their touch.
- I would make my favorite dish as my breakfast. I would cook for myself instead of running to the kitchen to boil some eggs or eat some flakes.
- I would then go to my office. On the way, I would feel the morning breeze with all my heart, I would watch the sky and trees. I would greet them back, which I have been missing for a long time.
- I would offer my place in the bus to some deserved person.
- I would try giving a hug to my best friend and listen to her in silence. Silence has been underrated for a long time between us.
- I would call my love just to tell him "I love you" for the final time. Dead painful it is not expressing the love.
- I would kiss my parents. I would make sure they have a comfortable life after my departure.
- I would call my good friends (5*1 min.=5 min.).
- I would donate all my organs and make sure the task gets done.
- I would donate all my clothes, books, and my best possessions by myself to someone who deserves it.
- I would have at least one meal with my family. We hardly ate together sitting at the same place. The gadget revolution bears the blame.
- I would only eat whatever has been cooked in my home.
- I would use my mobile as less as possible and would only use it to call people and would not engross into other application activities.

- I would genuinely thank God for the experience of the day. I have neither been experiencing nor thanking him for a long time.
- I would not just breathe. I would observe it for I know how valuable it is now (the less the availability, the more the value.)
- I would live the day, which many of us would not be able to do for many reasons.
- I would experience,embrace, and enjoy.
- I would receive and notice.
- I would give and learn.
- I would love.
- I would enjoy the essence of the pause in life.
- I would want to sleep in the lap of someone I love, talk to them about all the memories possible, and I would mark that as my last moment (last wish).

Wow. There are many more responses, but these just blew me away.

I would hope that any of us would want to make our last earthly moments to be heartfelt unions with all those that we love. I'm sure I'm not far off in my thinking.

Pressing issues would vanish. Our whole purpose in life would be to make things right and to be happy with the way we leave earth. Our outlook on relationships would pivot to grand encounters. We would spend less time in front of the TV and more time in front of the line at celebrations.

Think about the possibilities. Money would be less of a concern, and the sanctity of love would be in the forefront. We would greet each other with a friendly gesture and wish the other well. There would be no time for jealousy and even less time for hate.

If you are religious, you would spend more time pleasing your god and less time promoting your allegiance to a religion. The world would cease to be a burden as we begin to realize that we are just passing through. Why not live like that anyway?

In the Los Angeles area, there are a number of cemeteries that are home to the bodies of famous people:

- Hollywood Hills
- Forest Lawn Memorial Park
- Hollywood Forever
- Angelus Rosedale
- Chinese Cemetery of Los Angeles
- Evergreen Cemetery
- Rose Hills
- Mountain View

There are acres and acres of famous bodies spread all over the LA basin. You can visit the graves of Mickey Rooney and Toto. You can read how some are haunted and experience the history of a Vietnamese general and why he's buried there. You can stand on the site of famous TV and movie scenes. There's something for everyone.

Of course, the LA area is riddled with famous spots in these cemeteries used to act out a scene for our viewing pleasure. There are tours that will take you there and bring the dead to life.

Now, you might find these excursions disrespectful, and you might even wonder if they could be a little sacrilegious. But you have to admit, at least someone is visiting these graves. I'm sure some of you do visit your loved ones from time to time, but I'm positive that they would prefer that we do that while they are still breathing.

So keep your last day in mind from time to time. Think about how that day will look. Not the days after. Let the tour guides have those days.

I hope that we all have the chance to make our lives special. My hope for all of you is that you glide through life with ease and come out the other end with little baggage and lots of great memories. We are a complicated species. We tend to make everything harder than it needs to be. We see things that we think we need, but we miss the people that make us whole. We are all guilty of that. But we have a chance to make our lives mean something. We just need other people to make that happen. I'm not going to pretend that I am any different. I like to comfort myself with selfish ways and sometimes let relationships fade. I tend to believe that they will still be there when I want to reach out again. But what if they're not? What if I wait too long and miss those magical moments that they have to offer? I know, you may be thinking, "Well, it's a two-way street." Sure it is, and what if that street gets closed before I have a chance to travel down its two lanes again?

I have worked too many funerals to fall victim to that demise. I would like to think that I will feel complete when my journey ends.

CHAPTER 2

Last Day

There are two ways to be happy: improve your reality, or lower your expectations.

—Jodi Picoult

I live less than one mile from the gravesite of Cole Younger and his family. If you are not familiar with this famous outlaw, Cole was part of the James Gang. Jesse and Frank James partnered with Cole Younger and his brothers, Jim and Bob. They robbed banks and stagecoaches. And if you studied up on this band of bandits, you would find reasons for their madness. They were Confederate sympathizers. After the Civil War, Cole and his family wanted to get even for the poor treatment of Southerners by the hands of the Unionists. Their victims were all northern establishments, and they were considered heroes to the Southern states or territories. Believe it or not, Cole Younger died in March of 1916 as a free man. After his prison sentence was served, he traveled across the country lecturing about his life on the run.

We know more about some outlaws than we do some of our own family. I think about Cole Younger every time I drive past that cemetery. I sometimes wonder if his life would have been different if he was born in Minnesota instead of Missouri. Had Missouri not been (unofficially) accepted into the Confederate stronghold, would he have a different outlook toward the Unionists? Most interviews with him circled around his life on the run and less about who he really was. That was evident in an interview that he did with a journalist in St. Louis. The interviewer was warned not to ask any questions about the ex-guerrillas as many of them were still living. This interview took place in October of 1880, so there were many Civil War veterans still roaming around.

My point for bringing this outlaw into the conversation is to demonstrate how important it is to ask questions and to stay in touch with loved ones. History may not be of interest to you, but at least the history of your loved ones should be a reason to pry.

I have been involved with different aspects of the death-care industry for over twenty-seven years. There is none to be considered more important than the other. The grieving family cares little about the inner workings of how they arrive at a successful funeral service for your loved one as long as you do, and the deceased cares even less.

Over time, I have had the good fortune to work with some of the best in the field. I have also had the misfortune of working with some who care little about the needs of those left behind. But I can assure you that the good outweighs the bad by a huge margin.

My reasoning for bringing all this together for you is twofold. One, I wish everyone would stop and think about your last day on earth. Will you be happy with the person you have become? And did you have fun bringing your life to its final resting place? In other words, stop getting so uptight about your funeral plans and start realizing that you are not going to enjoy that day after all. Turn the agony of that last chapter over to someone who can relieve you of that burden. Maybe you just don't feel the need to plan for that last day. That is perfectly normal and respected. The best way to eliminate any burden of that morbid experience is to talk with your insurance agent or your local funeral home and get hooked up with a policy that fits your pocketbook and your family's needs. Most insurance policies that cover final expenses are cheap enough to do just that. That way, your loved ones are not left with a pile of worries on how to pay for your party in the sky. There's more about that in chapter 10.

Seek out funeral professionals in your area. Get to know them. Let them know you and your family. I know that this seems like a strange proposal, and I'm not suggesting that you walk into a funeral home and introduce yourself as their new best friend. No, I'm suggesting that you go to their website or call them and ask for information regarding final expenses. They will be glad to help. Keep in touch from time to time, and they will keep in touch with you as their policies and products change because one day, you and your family will need them. Chances are very good that a family member will ask you about your funeral plans one day. The younger you are, the less you care or even acknowledge the reality of that last day; but if you want to move on to better things and get that monkey off your back, take my advice. As you ponder this revelation, think about your parents or grandparents. How are they prepared? Are you going to be saddled with the burden of planning and paying? Have that conversation as soon as possible. (I will discuss funeral planning and options in another chapter.)

Focusing on life events and people that make you happy. This is the most important way to live your life. It lengthens your lifespan and strengthens your ability to deal with the everyday stresses of life's journey. But remember your obligations. If all the stars are aligned and the moon is full and Jupiter can be seen by the naked eye, then your obligations and the things that make you happy are the same.

When Mary and I were young and raising our daughter, Sarah,

I found myself in a constant ball of nerves trying to figure out how to pay for life's journey. I worked two jobs and kept coming up short. I finally decided that I needed to lift myself out of that rut and made the big move to head to college and work on a degree. Not knowing what direction I needed to follow, I sat with some folks at the local community college and decided to work toward a degree in communications. After a couple of semesters under my belt, I landed a job with a local TV news station and joined their production team.

I had the pleasure of working with local celebrities and even an occasional big-time celeb. I ran cameras and floor-directed from time to time. They do things in those studios a lot different today.

I was beginning to enjoy what I did for a living. That meant the world to me. The money wasn't pouring in like I wanted yet, but I was beginning to see light at the end of the tunnel.

After getting a little education under my belt and showing improvement in my ability to grasp the idea that commitment to a positive future can be achieved if I stay focused on the prize, I started to notice people were starting to take me seriously. Soon I was being asked to do things that I never imagined that I was capable of. I was asked to run the boards one night and was asked to do a satellite audio check with President Reagan. As I spoke to the president, I asked if he would speak so that our audio tech could balance his mic. President Reagan asked if I was in the building that he worked in when he was a sports broadcaster. I wasn't sure so I had to ask another tech. Turns out that we were in a different building, but that was a pretty cool conversation. After that night, I was ready for just about anything. I was still taking college classes and would use the news studio for study time. Knowing what angle to point a camera was becoming less of a chore as I would intuitively know what to do. Just as instincts will guide us to success if we let it, our ability to learn is never stifled. Birds instinctively know when to fly south and the north again. We should treat our daily lives the same.

Our instincts should tell us to take care of those issues so our loved ones are not saddled with that task.

An old friend once said to me that he could care less about his funeral and cares even less about who's going to pay for it. After all, he won't be here to deal with it. That was many years ago. We were young single adults, and both of us worried more about where our next beer was coming from than anything else. Well, the years have worn us both down, and as we have both melded into a family style of living, he, like myself, had grown to love the people that have surrounded him over the years. We grew to understand that we were not as invincible as we had thought and became more aware that others were the driving force behind our success and, for that matter, our reason for survival. My friend would eventually preplan his funeral and set up a rather lucrative expense release for his family.

I would like to believe that I would never be forced to adhere to a deliberate lifestyle, and I don't think that I am alone in my thinking. But I, like most, fall victim to the comforts of society's protection. That's not a bad thing. To be a member of the society that you are surrounded by gives you an outlet for your thoughts, your love, your vision for what can be and what is possible to improve our lives. To be a member of society puts us all on the same grade level and lets us share ideas. It is only natural to want to be near people who make your day better. It is a gift that we all accept and we all present without even knowing it. We understand that we each have a story to tell, a path to the end.

> *If there is a God, then he must be an artist and every man, woman and child represents a stroke of his brush. I can see our colors fold into that canvas as beauty and song. If we could step back and see the curves and abstract expressions intertwine into a gallery of our lives, then we shall know our place is with each other, and we shall feast upon a world filled with love for our fellow child of the brush.* (TK White)

In the years that I worked in the funeral business, I have met so many grieving family members who could recite volumes of history about their deceased loved ones and eulogizing them as "gone too soon"; but most seemed unprepared, even at a loss for thoughts. After all, the death of a loved one changes every aspect of your daily life. It will disrupt your routine; your heart will feel empty. Depending on the relationship you had with the deceased, you begin to realize that you must now change the way you approach your days ahead. I urge you to seek grief counseling if you are stricken with such a deep depression that you can't see the light at the end of the tunnel. But the one thought that seeps into the brain of a loved one left behind is simply this: *"Life is too damn short."*

I urge each and every one of you to be that person who, when you are gone, you made it hard for the preacher to keep your eulogy short. But more importantly, that you live long enough so that the chapters in your life have the proper lead into the final sentence of that last page. Don't be in a rush. Take care of yourself. There are people around you who love you and expect to see you tomorrow and in one piece.

Over the years, I have had the opportunity to know the lives of some great people. I have ministered many eulogies and have listened to countless stories of people who were loved and respected for who they really were.

I recall a funeral for a lady who lived just outside of Kansas City, Missouri. She was a well-known property owner in her community and loved nature. The land beneath her feet had a purpose. There were vegetable gardens and fruit trees. There were flower gardens and beautiful trees and walkways. She never sold her buds, but offered neighborhood folks to come and take what they needed.

She did what she loved. She had no immediate family as she was never married or had children. She died at the age of ninety-four. As the minister for her graveside service, I tried to reach out to what family she had so that I could offer up a respectable service for her. After numerous calls to reach someone, anyone who could give me some insight into her life, I was left with just the little information that was given to the funeral home by medical staff.

The service was short, but filled with an idea of how I envisioned her and her life. As there were just four people attending her service, I gave her a send-off that should have been heard by many more.

I think about her often. How can people be so inconsiderate to not pay their respects to someone so giving?

After a while, there would be a revelation that led me in a completely different avenue of thoughts on that subject.

It Just Wasn't Important

No, it made absolutely no difference to her. She never had to count her mourners or confront them. She lived ninety-four years, and most of those were shrouded in the glory of her favorite things. She prepared for her final day by preplanning her own service to the sky. She never worried about that day.

I guess the moral of her story is "keep yourself happy because you are the only one required to be at your funeral." It still bothers me when I think about her service. How lonely it felt and how utterly barren of a vision that leaves in my memory of that day. Empty seats filled with an echo of wind and leaves brushing against each other. That may have been her, letting us know that she was okay. It may have been a spirit of all the lonely souls that went before her, applauding her arrival to the heavens. I hope and pray that she was met with the love that was promised her on earth.

While living in Southern California years ago, I met a young man who, at the age of thirty-two, had never traveled out of the state. California is all he ever knew. He seemed interested in my descriptions of the four seasons while growing up in the Midwest. After a couple of years living in Southern California and its daily weatherless changes, I became aware of why he was so interested in the changes of the seasons. There is none in Southern Cal.

After I first became familiar with this young man, I surmised that he had a rather unhealthy approach to life. He and his wife were raising seven children from two previous relationships. He looked at life in a "survival" tunnel, I thought. He could never seem to ever make ends meet. He loved his kids, and he would do anything for them. He drove a broken-down old truck and was always in need of gas money. He had bill collectors knocking on his door all the time and sweated bullets every time his wife asked him to stop at the store on his way home.

The cost to exist in Southern California was and is hard for anyone under the level of the upper middle class, and he was not able to achieve a level above poverty. I could relate to his circumstances. If you remember, before I took matters into my own hands, many years earlier, I too was in distress and constantly scraping the bottom of the barrel to make ends meet.

I had offered suggestions to him, such as looking for work and home life in a less-expensive part of the country. He seemed to believe that there is nothing for him beyond the borders for Cali and would not take me seriously.

I stopped pressing him to look outside the box and let him wallow in his own desperate existence. Eventually, he would file bankruptcy and continue his trend to just get by. I learned a lot from him. I watched him look for ways to barely get by. He was a reminder to me to stay focused and work toward a happy and prosperous life. He worked hard to pay bills and feed mouths.

His headstone will probably read "Engraving Past Due." But he was in the glory of what made him happy—his family. Although I find myself in my own world of what makes me happy, the lesson is that we all have our own idea of what that is.

The problem is that the family that he so loves will be strapped with the burden of covering the cost of his funeral one day. Not only will they lose the one person that gave them a roof, food, and a warm bed, through all their grief, they will now have to pony up for his funeral expenses.

The lesson here is that it's sometimes not enough to love and provide while we are still together. If you truly love the ones you are protecting, protect them beyond the grave. Let them know that you are completely dedicated to their well-being. It could rub off. There could be a lesson for your entire family, that love and devotion stretches far beyond the heartbeat.

The human race is a strange lot. We complicate things, and we are too distracted by those complications. While a bear protects its cubs, we dress ours up and take pictures. While it is natural to be proud of our offspring, we tend to find ways to ignore them. We will set them in front of the TV or even hand them your cell phone and let them play games.

When we send them off to school each day, they are learning and growing up without you. They stop by friend's house on the way home from school; so by the time you see them, it's time for dinner, homework, and then bed.

We tend to think that there is plenty of time to interact with them, it doesn't have to be right now. As the years fly by, we start to realize that there is so much that we missed. From cradle to adulthood, we tend to miss everything in between.

So as we travel through time and write our own story, let's not forget the other humans that help make our story great. Spend as much time, face-to-face, as you can. Teach and be taught. Laugh and cry together. Don't let your last day on earth be a time of regret.

I overheard a young lady tell her friend about her mother. She was brilliant in her description of how her mom always made sure that her and her little brother got fed each day. I could tell that this little girl loved to talk about her mom. I hope she always will.

I remember writing obituaries for a local newspaper back in Iowa, many years ago. The editor set up with a template to help me fly through that mundane task.

McCall's - Honouring Life: Obituary Template

_____,_____(nee_____)
(Last name)   (Given name/nickname)

        peacefully
passed away   at _____ on _____
        suddenly

went to be with the/his/her Lord_____

at the age of ___ years/ in _____year.(or) Born
in_____ on_____.

Predeceased by _____

        his (loving) wife (of ____ years),_____;
Survived by
        her (loving) husband (of ____ years),_____;

Lovingly remembered by

sons, daughters, (or children); grandchildren, great-grandchildren; brothers; sisters; nieces, nephews, (may wish to include home city)

_____

_____

_____

_____

Background/Special thanks to

_____

_____

_____

_____

Visitation will be held at McCALL BROS. CHAPEL

on _____ at _____.

Every obituary started and ended the same. The only changes were, of course, the name, dates, and family left behind. This drove me crazy. I knew there was more to these poor souls than "She loved gardening" or "He loved fishing." Yeah, yeah, yeah. But what was he like? Was he inspirational? Did she guide anyone into a new way of living their lives? How did you feel when you were around them? Over time, I have met people who took the time to write their own obituary. This is usually the best way to make sure that your story is told through your eyes and not someone who might like to add some meat to the story or leave out important information. One that I read was less than complimentary to his widow, but as he put it, "what she was going to do, kill me?" Most people won't go through that trouble. They don't want to leave out important information or submit things that should not be brought up in a crowd of mourners.

I once wrote an eulogy for a farmer/WWII vet. I happened to know the family, and what I observed was how kind and helpful that family was. That mind-set had to start somewhere. Why were they kind? Did they learn this from him? They care more about helping others than most people that I have met. So as we sat and talked about his life, it became very clear that kindness and generosity was a family trait. They all learned from watching him and could see results while others returned that kindness.

Without getting into details about his eulogy, his kindness helped him save a life by putting himself in harm's way during the war. Now that's character. That's putting your mark on the world as a living, breathing angel. These are the obituaries that should be in print.

People live an entire life as a hero to someone. We are all guided by someone's influence, whether we know it or not. Our mannerisms, our good and bad habits, our very existence is somehow tweaked and adjusted to fit our personalities.

Strolling down the path of familiarity, comfort to the heart and soul. I brush with only charted territory. It seems to be the right path until another trail catches my eye. As I mix with new soil, like a bee's pollination of a different rose, only then can I grow and know that I am only a small part of a bigger picture. (TK White)

Ask the questions. Gain knowledge of other lives. You never know it could be your destination.

There are a lot of people responsible for molding me into the person that I am. That list changes from day to day, depending on who I meet. But I have life lessons that were handed to me from time to time that lifted me to another spiritual level. The inspiration from friends and family that challenge me to go farther. The smiles that I get when I am greeted makes me want to be a good friend. Everyone has and will have good and bad moments. I am guilty of allowing bad moments to ruin an entire day. A good friend of mine once told me that moments are made to fill a block of time in a day. Never let one block destroy the whole day. Work to correct that block then move on.

A fresh approach to weather a storm is to be the storm. Bring the wind and rain to your feet, and then you shall embrace its strength and fury. Never shy away from the aggressiveness of fear. If you face your challenges with a bold response, you will surely triumph. Being strong for you will make you strong for others.

I will talk about this in another chapter, but one of the concepts that keep me grounded is the Golden Rule: "Treat others as you wish to be treated."

It's a concept as old as the Bible and as effective as you would want it to be. Typically, we treat strangers better than we do the ones we love because we are unsure of what kind of reaction we would get from a stranger, but we have history with our loved ones and have seen their reactions.

Have you ever noticed that you will tell your friends things you would not tell your family? And you know that there are things you and your family know that you will not share with anyone outside of your tribe? It's natural to have a pipeline of trust for secrets and ideas. The key is to treat this as sacred grails. The secrets themselves are less important than the person you share them with. If you keep them, you keep your relationship strong. But you need to know if these are sacred enough to take to your grave. So have that conversation before it is too late. You will feel better for it.

The main road to the end of life is filled with ideas and imagination about the detours we think of taking. We are sometimes in too big of a rush to make decisions about the direction we follow. This is only natural because we are constantly asked about the path we choose.

The idea that your path can be shared with others sometimes escapes us. To know your loved ones fully is to take a journey along their path of life.

Working as a funeral home associate a few years back, I was assisting at a visitation for a lady with a family that you could compare to the Clampetts or the Duck Dynasty clan. They were a friendly bunch and displayed their grieving abundantly. Toward the end of the visitation, the granddaughter came to me and thanked me for being here for the family. All I really did was greet them as they arrived and handed out the service announcements. But I'll take a compliment when I can get it. She then went on to tell me that she was getting married the next weekend and it was sad that Grandma would not be there. I responded with some comforting words that she will be there in spirit. She continued the conversation by describing her upcoming wedding day presentation. With a smile on her face and a gleam in her eye, she pulled a toothless gentleman over toward us and introduced him as her daddy. As I extended my hand to give a friendly handshake, she excitedly described to me that she would be riding on the bed of Daddy's tow truck into the wedding ceremony. And then the groom and preacher would climb on and they would be married while Daddy drives down the gravel road.

Now, I give you this story as a reminder that there are stories in our lives that need to be told. Imagine this couple having children that never hear of their parents' wedding day.

Thinking about the last day on earth is not a thought that comes into the head of a busy person. It is something that creeps into your mind while meditating or relaxing in a quiet place. It takes time for the mind to muster up a scenario that would put the last day on earth toward the frontal lobes although we all have had that fleeting moment when our imagination takes us to that last day, that end moment. If we are normal, we fantasize about a glorified death. We die on the sword of an evil felon, or we explode into a million pieces while trying to save a distressed victim. We never dream of ever dying a slow death from cancer or heart disease. But unfortunately, that's how most of us will expire.

The truth is, your last day will be a lot more agonizing for your loved ones than for you. You might not have the time needed to make it easy on them, so make your plans soon.

Mary and Terrence White, May 31, 1980

CHAPTER 3

Supply and Demand

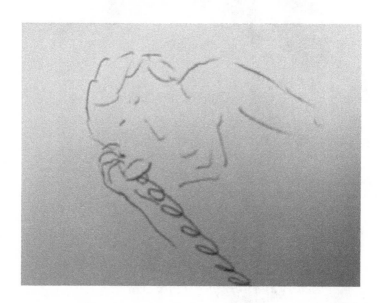

For a large amount of my time in the funeral world, I was on the supply side. I was a direct contact person for funeral homes and their purchase of caskets and urns. I really enjoyed that work, I think, because of the sense of knowing that a grieving family would be comforted seeing their loved one laid out in a beautiful casket from my inventory or have their ashes secured inside one of my beautifully engraved urns. I've had famous people resting in a casket that I picked out for them and some not so famous.

Famous or not, their lives interest me. I have always been fascinated by the lives of these souls for better or worse. Sort of like the old saying, "I ask children what they want to be when they grow up so I can get some ideas."

The dedication to serving the good funeral warriors in the world seemed overwhelming at times. There were deadlines and quality issues to caskets and urns. There were missed orders or orders that didn't get through a system. There were inventory backlogs and mislabeled products. And this was on a good day, haha.

Don't get me wrong, most days were not like this, but I wouldn't trade any of those bad days for nothing. Like any bad experience, I would learn from these. The key was having a team of people who loved their jobs. I was in awe of the work ethics of a lot of those folks in the supply line. The day seemed short, not just because of the heavy workloads but because of the magnitude of the love for the job they were doing. I kept, in the back of my mind, the loved ones that will be viewing their lost one and expected to send nothing but the best for their service.

The company that I worked for was a large publicly traded corporation. They have satellite locations all over the world. So working with teams in all these different locations, under one corporate flag, was, sometimes, mind-blowing.

Working out of the Milwaukee location many years ago, I received a call, one day from a funeral home owner looking for a hardwood oversize casket. At the time, the company I worked for was not producing oversize in hardwood, so I offered up a metal casket that was just the right size. He insisted that hardwood was the only way the family would go, explaining that the deceased had worked as a carpenter for most of his life.

I knew of a casket company close to Chicago that would custom build for you and so I gave him that phone number. About a week later, curiosity got the best of me, so I called my friend to see if my suggestion was valid. His voice raised as he chuckled a bit and then went into a play-by-play of that experience.

"Terry," he said, "your suggestion was perfect. They came out to our funeral home, measured our young man, and then headed back to Chicago to build a beautiful poplar oversize. It was stunningly beautiful, and they delivered it to us the next day. The funeral was a graveside service so we loaded the casket with the young man onto a flatbed truck. After all, he would not fit inside our hearse. The family met us at the cemetery. We had arranged for them to have ten pallbearers. We knew that it would take more than usual due to the size and weight of the casket and the deceased. There was only about six feet of carrying from the back of the flatbed to a waiting forklift that would take him the rest of the way. As we assisted the pallbearers, sliding the casket off the truck, you could hear a crack. And then just about six inches away from the lip of the truck, our friend ended up on the ground with the bottom of the casket under him.

"The pallbearers just stood there with the rest of the casket, still gripped and in shock. The gathered mourners all shrieked and screamed."

At this point of the story, I was beginning to think that this poor guy had to spend a lot of face time with his lawyer, so I asked him what happened after all that. He continued, "I stood there and started to cry, and then the entire family surrounded me, patted me on the back, and one of them said, "Don't you take this so hard. After all, it's not your fault he let himself go."

Wow. I was caught completely off guard by his story. I would keep this as a lesson in humanity, as some would have taken this opportunity to cash in on this unfortunate experience. We laughed and then I offered cheers for knowing there are good people still out there.

There were times when I would need to sit back at the end of the day and reflect on the day's experiences. Some were so bizarre that talking about them outside of the funeral biz, people would look at me like I was making these stories up.

I recall another experience receiving a phone call from a funeral director who wanted to bring a family to look at a couple of caskets. This was an unusual request because we were a "direct to funeral home" business and did not sell direct to consumers. But he was a trusted and longtime customer so I allowed it.

Soon after that call, two vehicles pulled up to the front of the building. One was a Town Car and the other was an older Chevy station wagon. My friend, the funeral director, exited the Town Car, and an older man and lady climbed out of the driver's side of the station wagon.

As all three of them entered, I greeted them at the door with my hand out. The older couple did not extend their hands so I shook my friend's hand as he gave me a look. You know that look, like "please help me."

Well, as it turned out, our older couple spoke very little English and seemed to want to just get this over.

They were from Armenia and were in the United States to bury a relative who had passed away in Milwaukee while fishing off the rocks at Lake Michigan. I had pulled a couple of caskets out of inventory and set them up for viewing.

They looked the both over and then selected the one they would purchase. The older gentleman handed my funeral director friend a roll of cash. He then asked if I would help them load the casket into their station wagon. I had them drive around to the back of the building and back into the oversized garage door. Once the wagon was parked where we needed it, I opened the back door and noticed an older lady's blue-haired head in the front passenger seat. I greeted her with a friendly hello but did not get a response. With the funeral director and the older gentleman on one side of the casket and me on the other, we loaded it into the back of the station wagon.

Of course, the casket was longer than the room needed in the back of that old wagon, so the old man reached into the back door area and pulled out a bungee cord. He then closed the door as much as he could and then hooked the bungee in place to keep the door somewhat closed. The couple climbed back into the driver's side of the wagon and off they went.

Well, it wasn't long after they headed out that I headed for home. I lived about a half hour south of Milwaukee, in Kenosha.

As I was driving down I-41, I noticed our friends in that station wagon driving in the far left lane. As I approached their vehicle, I noticed that the lady sitting in the passenger seat, next to the window, was not of the breathing type. I could tell that she had expired and was along for a ride to Chicago.

The next day, I called my funeral director friend and asked him if the lady in the front seat of the station wagon was supposed to be inside that casket. He told me she was, but the funeral was to be held in Chicago, and the family did not like my price to prepare the deceased for them and felt it would be best to have the funeral home in Chicago lay her out for them.

I have stories that would make your hair stand on end. From Texas to California and all the way north to Chicago and Milwaukee. But my favorite is the transitioning of a casket warehouse from the burbs to the caves.

I remember being crowned with the task of finding a new warehouse for our company's real estate group. This is a pretty big casket company with warehouses all over the world. The Kansas City location was a stand-alone building that was company owned. The powers that be thought it would be a better financial move to sell that building and move to a rented location. I didn't mind at all. It gave me time away from the office and let me see parts of the city that I never knew existed.

I would ride along with a commercial real estate broker about two or three days a week for a while and look at spaces that were available throughout the Kansas City area.

One day, the broker asked me if I had ever been inside the caves. Not being a KC native, I had no idea what he was talking about. So when he picked me up that day, we drove out to Independence and right into the mouth of a real cave.

Kansas City is well known for their underground warehousing as I was learning. This was just one of many throughout the KC region, and it took my breath away. There were miles and miles of road down in that cave. We drove for about two miles until we came to a warehouse location that he wanted to show me. After close inspection, we decided that this has to be our new home.

After months of build outs and plan changes, not to mention the task of moving hundreds of caskets and office furniture, we were finally in our new location.

It was about a month of operating underground that I was informed that our new home for our casket inventory was directly under a cemetery.

Kansas City is a pretty good-size metropolitan area, central to many industries. There are archives in these caves that belong to history, such as Harry Truman's writings and presidential library artifacts.

The IRS has files underground there. In fact, when they moved into a location next to our casket warehouse, there was talk of changing the name of our road to Death and Taxes.

Years of dealing directly with funeral home personnel has given me stronger faith in our human race. The men and women of this industry take it on the chin too often. Morbid rumors make their way into the mainstream, and then no one knows what to believe. Sure, there are stories that are true to a point, but just the nature of that business tends to add flavor to the sauce. Exaggeration is a natural component of any good story if you can get away with it. The stories I tell in this book are true, and I can verify each of them. Let's just say that some of this stuff, you can't make up.

Don't get me wrong, I like to exaggerate just like everyone else, but the key is to keep the meat of the story as true as it is.

In the early seventies, I had a friend everyone called Bones. We worked together at the JI Case Company in Davenport, Iowa, building tractors for road construction. Bones had a family of six kids, a wife, and an ex-wife who all lived under one roof. We would tease him often about his commune arrangement, but deep inside, I envied him for his determination for keeping peace with his environment. Bones made me realize that life can be good or bad, it is all up to me and how I react to any moment.

I encourage everyone to write down your memories and keep them close to you. My friend Bones and his family is a good example of why I keep these memories close. He was a big part of me growing as a person. Through life, I have learned to react to situations as they greet me. I never dreamed that I would be a part of so many others' last day and at their threshold over to the heavens, but there I was killing it.

I recall the day that I received the order for the casket to be delivered for a very well-known pop artist.

Shortly after that call, I was receiving another for the arrangement of a casket for one of America's favorite Charlie's Angel. That was in June of 2009. The funeral homes for them were in opposite directions of the LA grid, and both were to be delivered at the same time on the same day. As you can imagine, these were high-alert deliveries. The press was alerted to both locations, and my instructions were to deliver them in unmarked vans or trucks. If you were alive then, you probably noticed that the TV newspeople were totally obsessed with the death of the pop star and not so much with the angel. The pop star died from an overdose of benzodiazepine, and Charlie's Angel died after battling cancer for three years. There are parts of this day that I am not allowed to put here in print, but the takeaway here is that our actions and decisions that we make throughout our lives have consequences. While the press was obsessed with the pop star's death, they were also not so kind to his legacy. A bright musical genius that entertained the world with his music and choreography was eulogized by the press as a drug-ridden child molester whose family was trying, desperately, to make sense of his death.

Charlie's Angel, on the other hand, was described as a loving actress and model, with a family that mourns her death in peace as she lies in state as a fraction of the woman that left us with so many great memories. A poster of her that hung in the bedrooms of every teenage boy of her time would pop up on the tube every now and then. But the focus was clearly on one and not the other. His funeral was a sellout, and hers was attended by family only.

There was no comparison between the two funerals or coverage of each. If the question ever arises of what famous person passed away the same time as our pop star, most would not know the answer.

So as the coverage of one overshadowed the other, the question is, how would you want to be remembered? More importantly, how do you want your loved ones to remember you?

I sometimes feel sorry for celebrities. They have no secrets or privacy outside their homes. The press is not always kind to them and sometimes get a story wrong. That seems to be the price of fame. It is also a huge reason so many turn to mind-altering drugs and alcohol.

I recall the day I sold my first oversized wood casket. It was for a particular celebrity who died from an overdose. He was a well-known comedian and loved by many. One of his good friends said that he always had to be on his game. Wow, what a burden that would be. Every day, he was expected to be the funny guy. What a relief it must have been for him to have an outlet to help him express his talent.

Fortunately, most of us are not celebrities. We are more likely to feel that pressure at work alone, not at home or on our way to the hardware store. We have freedom to move about the earth without feeling like we are on display everywhere we go.

My idea of everlasting love is to be prepared for that last day, whether you are a celebrity or a plumber. We have the means to help our loved ones through the agony of losing us. The last day will come. It always does. Show your love every day till then.

Make It Snappy

The one aspect of the supply side of the funeral business was that sense of urgency. It seemed that three-fourths of the orders that I took, over the years, were orders that needed to be filled *now*. For seventeen years, I wondered how it became such a rushed business. After all, Gramma wasn't going anywhere.

It wasn't until I worked in the funeral homes as a funeral associate that I began to understand that sense of urgency. My first encounter with making sure that the family would be comfortable and pleased with every aspect of their loved one's funeral was a complete eye-opener for me. In just about every case, the funeral director was strapped with all the weight of making a bad situation into a loving and beautiful occasion. It starts with the phone call from the family member pleading with the funeral home to take good care of Mom. Then there's the removal of the body from their home or hospital or nursing home or sometimes the county morgue.

Then comes the meeting with the family to discuss the funeral arrangements and cost. If you can imagine working with loved ones who just lost a huge part of their lives, hoping that they can keep it together long enough to make sound decisions regarding the upcoming pageant to celebrate the life of their deceased loved one, and do this on a daily basis with different families who have different ideas about that journey to the other side, only then can you grasp the magnitude of the proper psychology that it takes to be at the receiving end of the end of life for the rest of us.

This is usually the part that forces the urgent need for the supplier to step up their game. During the family visit, it is determined when and where to hold the funeral.

Now, if you have ever been in that room, talking with a funeral director, then you know the feeling. You want Mom to have the pageant of a lifetime, and you want it to happen *now*. You know there will be family and friends coming into town from all over the country, but you want this gig to be done and over, hoping that the finalization of seeing Mom lowered into the ground will help you heal faster.

There's also the prep and embalming that has to be scheduled and the selection of the casket, or if she is going to be cremated and what would they like to have engraved on the urn. There's the scheduling of a grave opening and closing and, of course, the headstone.

So let's say the family decides that they want a Friday funeral and this is Wednesday. That means that they also want a Thursday evening visitation. The embalmer needs to be scheduled, the casket needs to be ordered, the makeup and dress needs to be scheduled. Associates need to be scheduled to man the service. The minister needs to be alerted and sit with the family so they can present a proper eulogy. Incoming flower arrangements need to be properly placed, and music needs to be set up and ready for play. The announcements need to be written and printed. The obituary needs to be presented to the funeral home website and the local paper. If there's a graveside service, cars are fueled up and ready, and the grave needs to be opened and properly set up for a service. A death certificate needs to be ordered, and let's not forget that the casket better be perfect, with no scratches, dings, or dents. The funeral home needs to be clean, and the parking lot free of litter. If this is a military service, you better have someone there who knows the proper way to fold a flag and place it on a casket.

The venue needs to be presented with seating reserved for family and pallbearers. A church truck needs to be available, its wheels in working order.

Now, imagine if you had multiple funerals scheduled for the same day. Think about the magnitude of scheduling and follow-up it takes to coordinate a day like this.

Keep in mind that this is not a business that can easily predict how their business is going to flow. A funeral home is not a 7-Eleven. They can't know how to fill their shelves with products or man their registers with warm bodies. They could go weeks or months without a case.

A normal funeral home will have a roster of associates, licensed funeral directors, embalmers, makeup and dress people, office personnel, celebrants, and an army of others to keep the place clean, motor police, and the list goes on. Keep this in mind when you are across the table from a funeral director when he or she slides the price over to your side of the table.

According to NFDA (National Funeral Directors Association), there were 19,136 funeral homes in the United States by the end of 2019. That is down from 20,557 in 2009. Just ten years earlier, that is a figure that includes a large number of homes that have been acquired by large conglomerates. In some cases, these big companies will purchase a funeral home and then close the doors after a short operating timeline. After all, to them, it's just business.

The good news is that these big companies do keep personnel from the homes that they buy. These are usually the best of the best. You will probably never know the difference when you walk into one of these, and I'm not at liberty to tell you about them or I could find myself in hot water. The point is that there will continue to be fewer and fewer homes in the future, so get to know the people inside. They are the ones that will guide you to the right grave.

The average NFDA-member funeral home handles 113 calls per year and has three full-time and four part-time employees.

See the following cost statistic:

National Median Cost of an Adult Funeral with Viewing and Burial: 2019 vs. 2014

Item	2019*	2014*
Nondeclinable basic services fee	$2,195	$2,000
Removal/transfer of remains to funeral home	$350	$310

Embalming	$750	$695
Other preparation of the body	$255	$250
Use of facilities for viewing	$425	$420
Use of facilities for funeral ceremony	$500	$495
Hearse	$340	$318
Service car/van	$150	$143
Basic memorial printed package	$175	$155
Metal casket	$2,500	$2,395
Median cost of a funeral with viewing and burial	**$7,640**	**$7,181**
Vault	*$1,495*	*$1,327*
Total with vault	*$9,135*	*$8,508*

2014 prices have not been adjusted for inflation.
* Median price – The amount at which half of the figures fall below and half are above.

Of course, the actual cost will depend on coordinating and cooperation from outside sources, such as casket and urn suppliers, cemetery personnel, vault suppliers and setup people, chemical suppliers, and let's not forget the tech who keeps those vehicles running.

So for $7,640, spread out over a tremendous number of people and products, not to mention utilities and fuel and cleaning staff, you can say goodbye to your loved one with dignity and pride.

The one element that is not mentioned here is the cost of a minister or as the funeral world would prefer to present the eulogy orator as a celebrant.

The celebrant will usually cost in the neighborhood of $150 to $250.

I prefer to charge $0. That's right, I said zip, not a penny. I believe that families have too much to worry about without the weight of another bill. When I sit with a family, I feel that it is important that they feel at ease and not to measure the time and cost to properly offer up a lifetime of memories for someone they will never have a chance to visit with again. That's not to say that I have never received tips. I have and those are appreciated, but not required. Knowing what the family is going through, emotionally and financially, gives me great honor to know that I will be a part of their salute to their loved one.

Having worked the good work as a funeral associate, and followed some of the best funeral directors in the business, it gives me great pleasure to be a part of the healing process.

Now let me qualify my generosity. I do not have a parish to concern myself with. There are no stained glass windows that need cleaning or even a church to put them in. I am a nondenominational minister. I will talk more about that in chapter 10.

There's a tradition among funeral professionals. We will keep one of the printed memorials for every funeral that we work. This is not to put a notch in our holster but to give thanks and a celebratory nod to the life that we were fortunate enough to present a pageant for. These memorials remind us of the souls they represent and the journey they traveled to be where they are. Some call that heaven.

I have inspected caskets that were to be used for presidents and caskets that were to be used for indigent cases. I never felt that one was more important than the other. Hell, the casket for the president will be covered with a flag anyway. But I still made sure it was just as nice as the one for the homeless guy. There's a code of ethics that funeral professionals follow. Respect for the families and the deceased must never waver. There will always be a circle of protection for them through the hands of a true funeral professional.

There were times when it seemed that the dignity of that profession was hard to hold in place. One of the strangest things that happened during my time in Southern California was asking an employee who had been working there for many years before I came along why this busload of people kept driving through our parking lot about twice a week for a while. He told me that the tour buses come by every now and then to show people where the casket came from for some celebrities. Wow.

Now, there was the occasional order from a funeral home that wanted us to deliver to one of the studios in Burbank, and from time to time, an agent from a studio would stop by to look for a special casket or urn. One such agent looked over one of our urns like he was in the market for a diamond ring for his sweetheart. This guy was a little strange and sat with me in my office for about an hour to discuss the type of funeral products he was looking for. I let him talk for a while before I reminded him that we won't be doing business without the expressed uses of a licensed funeral home. That was our policy. We only sold to and delivered to licensed funeral homes. He said that that is no problem and explained to me that when the time arrived, he would have an associate from a funeral home contact me for an order. The next day, we received an order for six caskets and fourteen urns to be delivered to a certain studio. I called the owner of that funeral home and reminded him that we can only deliver to him and that he needed to make arrangements to have the products delivered to the studio. Now, I tend to bend the rules from time to time, but this was a large order that had quite a price tag attached. The owner gave me the name of a guy at our corporate office and told me that he already gave permission to make the exception. After explaining to him that his friend at our corporate office had left the company a year ago, he decided that he would rent a truck and pick up the caskets and urns the next day.

Well, that order never got filled; but over time, we did have our products used for certain TV episodes and a movie or two, but the best request came to me from a porn studio that happened to be right next door to our warehouse. I think I had been in place there in Southern Cal for about three years before I knew that there was a porn studio next door. One afternoon, as I was leaving for lunch, there, in front of my office, was a guy selling DVDs of porn. As I walked past him, I recognized him and said hi. When I got back from lunch, I told one of my associates that I saw our neighbor out front selling porn DVDs. She informed me that he was the guy who ran the porn studio next door. I pretended that I already knew that and moved on.

It almost never rains in Southern California, but when it does, it pours. It was a rainy afternoon, and I was watching someone under an umbrella running toward the front door of our offices. A few moments later, my administrative assistant called me to tell me that our next-door neighbor needs to see me ASAP. I knew who she meant. It was our porn studio guy. Well, I figured that this had to be one for the books so I invited him into my office, had him take a seat, and asked, "What can I do for you?" His response was quick: "I need to borrow a casket." I guess that I was a little disappointed, and it must have shown on my face. I really thought he was going to ask if he could use our warehouse for shooting a scene. Now, I would have said no, but how cool would that be just to get asked? No, he wanted a casket. I had to turn him down but gave him the number of another casket company that might step up for his needs. He left in a huff and never spoke to me again.

Later that year, my night-shift folks told me that the porn studio moved out overnight and even stopped over to ask if they could borrow one of our trucks. Not that I didn't trust my night-shift personnel, but I did take inventory of our fleet and checked mileage.

Because sometimes cash talks, but I can report that everything checked out okay.

It wasn't too long after our friends moved that I began to notice that the tour buses no longer stopped by. Hmmm.

Speaking of rain, Mary and I loved Southern California. We visited the beaches on many occasions and spent a large part of our time just driving around and checking out the sights. One trip was to a little berg called Solvang, a town just off the 101, north of LA into the corners of wine country. We visited Solvang a few times. It's filled with little shops and wine tasting. But there was a calmness about that town that sparked my attention. I loved to just find a bench and let Mary walk her way around the little town. I was intrigued by the cleanliness of the air and the crisp cool breeze. It always made me think of the spring afternoons in my hometown of Davenport, Iowa. Growing up in Davenport was pretty calming compared to other places around the country. We were Midwesterners and never locked our doors. Our parents kept the car keys in their car, and our bicycles sat in the front yard and never got stolen.

I would daydream as I sat there on that bench. Now most people would use that time to watch people. Not me. I daydreamed. I would get so deep into my thoughts that I sometimes forgot where I was until one day I was sitting on the bench, just about to drift off, when a guy and his buddy sat down and started talking. I wanted to tell them to find another bench, but that would be rude. So I listened to them gab. Then my ears perked up as one of them explained that Alfred Hitchcock's daughter, Patricia Hitchcock, lives right here in Solvang. Now, most people would get excited and kinda starstruck by that news. I got irritated. Yes, irritated. I enjoyed my trips back to never-never land, and I didn't need reminding that every damn corner of California was riddled with someone who needs to be recognized. Wow. Did I need a vacation from vacation land? You bet I did.

While I enjoyed my time in Southern California, I was pretty overwhelmed with a workload that I was not used to. The death rate in California is something that I wasn't prepared for. California has the largest number of deaths per year than any other state. In the

Midwest, we would prepare for the usual increase in deaths at the start of winter. In the land of fruits and nuts, it was always that time of year. At times I wanted to just stop the presses and start over. But there was no time for that. I tried to emulate my way of doing business in the Midwest, but it was just too slow and laid-back. To keep up with the flow of the death rate, I needed to be on a different level of urgency. In order to be proactive and prepared for the unexpected, I was constantly on call and taking calls at all hours of the day and night. I was fortunate enough to have a staff who became used to the pace and was always there to support me.

My sense of urgency was overshadowing my sense of kindness. I became angry at times and would lash out at whoever was close enough. I was charged with inventory at seven warehouses and a manufacturing unit, a fleet of trucks, a paint booth that required the local EPA visits and the constant badgering from OSHA, misbehaved employees that required conferences from corporate HR, local law enforcements constantly ticketing my trucks for parking on the streets, and a multimillion-dollar budget. I was constantly on the phone with the sales department, the logistics department, the manufacturing department, the finance department, funeral homes, and landlords. And to top it all off, I'm having chest pains.

It was mid-May in 2009. I have been running nonstop for some time, and my worry level was going through the roof. My wife, Mary, needed a break from me. We still owned our home back in the Kansas City area, and our daughter Sarah was staying there and paying us rent. It was time for Mary to take a break from grouchy old Terry and go visit Sarah and some old friends back in the Midwest. While she was gone, I checked myself into the hospital for chest pains. I didn't want Mary to know and worry, and that's why I needed her to go when she did. I was put through a series of tests and could not find a reason for my chest pains, so they decided that I was suffering from heartburn and put me on something for that. Over time, I would continue to have the occasional chest pain, and I would just blow it off as heartburn.

When Mary returned a few weeks later, it was like a breath of fresh air brushing over me. I started to relax a little and feel a little better. The days would continue to be overwhelming, and there were days that I would just walk away and find a place to unwind. The chest pains continued, and I was beginning to believe that I was misdiagnosed by the medical staff at the hospital. There were times when I thought that this last promotion was a huge mistake. I could have bitten off more than I could chew. The company had a tough time filling this spot, and I was beginning to understand why.

I made some phone calls to past managers and got their feedback regarding their experiences at the helm of this machine that we call the casket distribution network. It all started to come together. The pains in my chest were real and familiar. I needed a break.

As much as Mary and I loved Southern California for its mild weather and beaches, it was time to move along. I was preparing myself for the ultimate change of lifestyle. I was going to talk to my boss and suggest that I look somewhere else for employment. That my mind-set has sunken into an abyss of negative matter and I am taking quite a bath with my health. And then my phone rang. It was my boss. He talked for a bit and thanked me for all that I do and then asked if I would be interested in moving to a smaller market and down to just one warehouse to manage. It's like he heard every word that I was thinking.

The compassion surrounding death becomes overshadowed when the number gets so great. I have always felt that the love and anguish surrounding the loss of a loved one should be accentuated for all to grasp and take to heart. Operating a machine that just keeps pounding out products for cash is not my idea of bringing home the love. While I understand the reality of profit against operating cost, I also tend to consider what these products mean to the end user and their loved ones. Don't get me wrong; this company took pretty good care of me over the years, and I will never forget that, and I understand the need for the greasing of the production wheel, but losing my compassion for the sake of profit is not in my DNA.

I continued with this company, but in a different location for a short time.

I found myself in Houston, Texas, and sweating like a fat kid at a pie-eating contest. I had more time on my hands and was starting to have fewer chest pains. Then one day, walking through a local department store, I blacked out and hit the floor. When I woke up, I was surrounded by employees of the store. One was holding my glasses, and another was holding my shoes. My arm hurt because I fell directly on that arm and I was having a tough time standing back up. One of them told me that I was just walking, and she watched me just collapse. She asked if I wanted medical attention and I refused. I left the store concerned that I may have bigger issues than chest pains. I thought about checking myself into a hospital but didn't. I went back to my apartment and sat there wondering if this was the end. Mary was back in Kansas City and completely unaware of my troubles. For now, that's the way I wanted it. The less she knows, the less she has to worry.

After a confrontation with a member of the corporate human resource department, I retired from that company in the next few weeks and loaded everything up in a U-Haul and moved back to Lee's Summit, Missouri. I was sad because for seventeen-plus years with a company that brought me in touch with so many wonderful people and gave me opportunities to succeed at so many levels, I was moving on. The good news was that I finally felt free. I no longer had to worry about someone else's overtime or a scratch on a casket or trucks breaking down or a funeral home needing special assistance with expensive time deliveries. All of that just went away. For the first few days back in the KC area, I continued to have chest pains and then, within a month of being back home, I had the big one. The heart attack that changed everything. I would become the burden to my wife and daughter that I always hoped I never could be. They nursed me back to health and was so wonderful to me that I began to realize that I was never ready to be at the helm of a machine that spits out products as fast as they sell. I was meant to comfort those who need to let their loved ones go.

To some, a job is just a job. To others, a job should be part of who you are. If you hate who you are becoming, think about a different path. Don't work just for the money. If the job kills you, you can't spend a dime. My parents worked to put food on the table, and they were rarely in a good mood. If that is the meaning of life, no wonder depression is at an all-new high. Here's a good indicator for you: if you hate Sundays because Monday is just around the corner, you might need a different job. The truth is, your lifespan depends on your happiness.

There were moments that were springboards to eye-opening realities for me. The people that I met over the years in this industry taught me to listen and grasp the heart of those in need. I was introduced to a couple of funeral directors that spent their free time feeding the homeless in Southern California. We spoke often, and they would invite me to join them during funeral services for such folks. The number of these cases would tie me up in knots. I wondered what happened to their families. How did they fall so low? Most of the cases that I was introduced to were folks with faltering mental problems and some who fell victim to drugs. There was a huge number of homeless veterans who were suffering from PTSD so bad that you couldn't keep them in a controlled environment. These funeral directors would use their own money to help them. And when our friends met their demise, these heroes would use what the state offered to pay for their burials; but it is, however, California, and the cost to do a respectable service is pretty high. Today, according to CalVCB (California Victim Compensation Board), they will offer up to $7,500. This is a fund that is designated to victims of violent crimes. So it is hard to get justifications in many cases of indigent deaths. There are no funds set aside in the state of California, but each county may have a particular program that can be used. According to *funeralwise.com*, Los Angeles County, for example, has a program that pays for cremation expenses; but if a loved one wants to claim the ashes of their deceased family member, they will need to pony up an additional $350 to $470.

Knowing all this, these funeral heroes will help their (friends of the street) out by using their own funds to provide a respectable service. Now and then, they will need someone to step in and provide the eulogy. In most cases, these heroes will be that celebrant. That's when I became interested in the true meaning of a ministry. I was completely in awe of these funeral heroes. They never asked for handouts and would rely on their own fortunes to give where it mattered to them.

Through the years, as a supplier to the world of the death-care industry, I became immune, at times, to the actuality of death. A phone call became just an order for one of my products. A special delivery to a funeral home became an expense instead of a need. I began to become a part of a culture that did not include my expectations of filling the needs of others.

There will be moments of clarity in the days to come. My heart was about to transport me to a place where I belong.

CHAPTER 4

Great Idea

Growing up, I had always been interested in a variety of professions. I can recall, at a very early age, say, around four or five, our neighbor who would stop over to visit my parents. He was a highway patrol officer. His badge seemed so big that I would stare at it the whole time he was there. I dreamed of being that guy.

There were other inspiring moments to rattle my future professional paths, but like most dreams, they were just passing moments. Over time, I had fantasized being a doctor, fireman, professional musician, TV news anchor, actor, politician and even the CEO of a major corporation. Not once, did I assume any one of these would actually materialize. They were dreams, but I held onto them for a while, as I was grooving through my real professional paths.

I was a baker, a stamp clerk, and even a news camera operator. I wrote obits for a newspaper and drove a shuttle van. I delivered beer and mixed paint. I worked in department stores and construction sites. There were times that I milled parts in a factory for tractors and times when I sold insurance. I owned a bar, I drove trucks and sold cars, and there was a time when I pumped gas. But my heart and soul always fell to the feet of helping others through difficult times.

What the funeral industry did for me was open my eyes to the realization that we leave here with nothing in tow but for and from the love of ourselves and others. That all those years, months, weeks, minutes, and seconds that make up our journey can either be filled with good or bad. That is our choice and perspective.

I have had the honor to minister eulogies for a variety of souls, from accountants to farmers and even young ones who lost their way. I took the time to sit with family and discuss the years and journeys of their loved ones. I never had any family member or friend recall a negative moment throughout the history of their deceased loved one. They talked of humorous moments, of fun trips. They talked of how loving and kind Mom was or how helpful Dad became to his community and to them. They gleaned with inspirational thoughts of how Gramps made them feel and the memories of Christmas with Grandma and family.

Never assume that you are less important than anyone else. The stories I've heard over the years gives credence to the idea that we are all loved.

Sometimes, we get too involved with our fears to see that. Sometimes, I had the feeling that all the members of the human race come with a certain amount of good, and I don't think that I am wrong.

I remember attending a service for a dear friend in Kansas City. Like most funerals, there was the standing in line to greet the family, shake a lot of hands, and hug a lot of grieving souls. We reminisced about all the fun we had in years past. There was laughter and tears. It was like a reunion of sorts and the occasional "Let's not wait for a funeral to do this again" talk. Truth was, there were a lot of good emotions going around, and I could tell that everyone needed that time to visit.

When the service started, I sat with my wife Mary and my daughter Sarah and bent my ear to receive what I wanted to hear, a good old life story about my dear friend. I waited through the Lord's Prayer and the reading of those left behind. I managed to keep my interest as the minister would find more prayers to read and how one or another would remind him of a story that had nothing to do with the guy laid out in that casket behind him.

He went on and on about stories in the Bible and the path that the Lord offers each of us. I began to realize that this guy knew nothing about our friend who had moved on to another world.

He didn't know that this guy could shoot a fly off a fence post with a rubber band. He didn't know that my good buddy was one of the best fishermen I ever knew. He didn't know how much he loved his kids and grandkids and the stories that he would tell them. He did not know my friend.

It was clear that he did not take the time to talk with family and learn about the pain he felt the day he was on fire or the ups and downs of his relationships throughout the years. I had a sick feeling that my friend was not getting the respect he deserved.

I vowed that day that I would never let that happen with any eulogy that I deliver. I vowed that I would do what it took to know the deceased and offer a respectful service.

It matters not who we are. Each and every one of us will have only one last day. We will be met with that moment of truth. Our last breath will be the period at the end of our life story. We all have a story to tell. Don't believe for a second that yours is less important than mine or anyone else's.

"Bring it home," a well-inspired saying when someone is on the home stretch. It's used at sporting events and concerts. I like to use it during a service for the deceased. It helps me organize my thoughts and align a respected eulogy.

Growing up, I was taught that the minister was just the guy that preaches every Sunday. I was under the impression that a minister would raise his hands and voice to the heavens so that the rest of us can have a look at what glory should be. But over time, I have learned that a real man/woman of the spirit is one who listens and guides. One who tries to see things from the talker's perspective. One who will help you through your troubled times, and one who will celebrate with you for your achievements. A good minister should be comfortable in your home and see your family as theirs.

I like to look at the life of my friends who left us as a marathon of sorts. There's hills and twists and turns that are riddled throughout the course of life. There are potholes and roadblocks and moments when we are forced to stop and look both ways.

Sometimes we don't even know what our destination will look like. Sometimes we take shortcuts because we do.

It's that journey that I'm interested in. I want to know what got you to your last day. What got you to the end of your journey? Were you cautious? How did you deal with the roadblocks of life?

After sitting through eulogies that never caught the essence of the poor souls who lay in state, enough times, I sometimes want to say something to that preacher. I'd like to know what ever happened to their compassion for the family and the deceased. Why would they even bother getting out of bed that day if all they were going to do was read an obituary that was written by someone else and then a handful of prayers?

Funerals are meant for celebration of life. It is a time to remind the mourners of the life that ran a marathon through streets filled with potholes and roadblocks. I can only imagine a poor soul looking down upon their funeral service, only to discover that there is no recognition for the life they lived. You can see it in the mourners' faces. They seem distracted and confused. They wonder to themselves, "Why am I here? When will this be over?"

Oftentimes, the celebrant is the pastor of the church that the family recognizes as the representation of their faith. If the eulogy is less than descriptive of the life of the deceased, then it seems pretty obvious that they probably missed a few Sundays along the way. Regardless of a family's absentee report at the temple, it is the job and obligation of the pastor to see to it that your loved one gets a respectable send-off.

As a funeral associate, I have witnessed some wonderful services as well, designed to encapsulate a life that would make anyone proud to know the deceased. I recall a service in Independence, Missouri, on a Saturday morning. The chapel was filled with mourners. We had to add folding seats at the back and through the doors.

The pastor began the service like any other, with a prayer and a reading of family left behind and those who went before. And then like a bolt of lightning, he started to describe a life that brought even the staff to take notice. There was not a face in the crowd that was not focused on the pulpit. There was laughter and tears. At the end of each pew lay a box of tissue. Standing at the back of the chapel, it was like watching collection plates being passed around as those boxes would go from side to side.

That person lying there so peacefully in that casket came to life. It was clear as ice that respect was placed properly at the resting place. By the end of that service, we all became a member of that family, but for just a day. It was magical. We all rode along as he directed us through the streets of a life that twenty minutes earlier I never knew.

I thought to myself, this is the way everyone should be eulogized. A true celebration of a life from start to finish and all the stops in between.

Now, you must understand that it is hard to capitalize on the important events of anyone's life in such a limited amount of time. It takes time to know the life of someone. That is why it is so important to sit with family members and try to understand a person's life. The more people you talk to, the closer you will get to the real person. When one reflects on the magic of their loved one, another will give another angle to that same magic, for example, "She never had to say what she felt, you could see it in her facial expressions" and "You can take one look at her and know she was mad."

Pay attention to the little things. They might see them as little things, but they all add up to one wonderful loved one.

No matter who enters or leaves my life, I have had the honor of knowing who they are. Some I would invite back in; others, well, let's just say I'm glad they're gone.

It's a mystery to us why we are attracted to some and not others, why we seem to gather around a certain type of personality and why we feel the need to have them in our lives. Some believe that it is God's plan and that our meeting others is no mistake or random in his kingdom. Others see it as an attraction of chemistry. I won't pretend to know the truth. Because you can also make the argument that God is the creator of chemistry. Some might see that as "Who came first, the chicken or the egg?" The truth is that it makes no difference who came first. What's important is that we are here now. Let's make the best of it.

I remember my first week in Kansas City. Everyone at the facility that I would be in charge of were great except for one. From the first day we met, you could tell that he had no love for me and really questioned why I was chosen to run this ship. There would be days when I would have to reprimand him for not following company policy or unrelated overtime. He acted as if he wanted me to challenge him every time. As time went on, our relationship never improved, and he would eventually move on to other employment. Nothing I did or said ever helped to close that gap between us. We never met before I arrived there so it had nothing to do with past experiences. So I just have to chalk that up to bad chemistry. Oftentimes, I will catch myself working too hard to make a connection. I do understand that there will be times when that is just not possible and I must move on.

Think about the meet and greet at work on a Monday morning. In many cases, the question will come up about your weekend. While this is probably just a rhetorical greeting in passing, sometimes it is fun to use that as an opportunity to describe something that happened that needs to be broadcast—an awkward encounter or a newfound love, a disastrous weather incident or a new purchase. You never know, your story could give an opening for someone to talk about something that needs to be said. I try to stay open to conversations, so let's talk.

Any way you want to describe it, we seem to be connected in some ways. Let it happen. Let your adventure take you to another level. You would be surprised how many others think like you and have a need to talk or even just hear someone else describe their thoughts.

Think about your last day as the end of a marathon. Think about it as the last page of the last chapter of your life. You can start today to make that journey one for the record books. Treat others like they are family. Treat each day as if it needs a theme. When asked to help someone, do so with a smile on your face and appreciate that they asked you.

When you see someone in distress, ask what you can do for them. Put that dollar in that cup of that guy on the corner. Feed him. Help him keep warm. Do the good deed, and the good deed will come back to you tenfold. Write down the things you want to do and accomplish and make a list of the people you want to be happy with. Take the time each day to thank God or your lucky stars that you were able to take in the glory of life for today. Then get prepared for tomorrow.

The heaviest thing that you want to unpack in that baggage to your grave is regret. Now you may move about the world and fill your baggage with gleaming memories.

I'm never sure if I want to turn left or right. But one thing is for sure, any way I turn, from now on, will be a new adventure. I no longer stress about the world at my feet. I know that there will always be circumstances that I have no control over, but the one that I do have control over, I can handle.

One step we can all take is to never let time get in the way of a good visit. Right now, we are living in a strange time. COVID-19 has stifled our lifestyle. But we are not going to be in this jungle forever. When this virus has gotten under control, we need to visit more and communicate more. There is no better visit than in person. I have talked with people who are devastated because their trips to Disney had to be canceled or a cruise had to be dropped. If you listen to a lot of these, you will notice that a visit to a long-lost friend or relative was not part of the plan. It's interesting that when we make plans for that free time, it's not to hook up with someone you haven't seen in a while.

Most of the time, people don't take real vacations. They take time off to work on the house or babysit grandkids or make a little cash on the side. I know that we tend to treat our free time with repairing things and not ourselves. I am just as guilty. Owning a home will force you to do things that you wouldn't have to do if you were renting. But it was a choice you made, and you're sticking to it.

Here's some ideas for you and your family to discuss that will help clear your head and get back to feeling the love:

1. Make a list of the people you want to visit.
2. Decide on vacation days to use as visiting days.
3. Make a list of the things that need to get done around the house.
4. Decide on times you need to take care of these.
5. Make a list of places you would like to visit.
6. Decide on vacation days to use for these places.
7. Take some time for yourself and stick to that schedule. (Meditation).

My wife and I know people that we want to visit all over the country. We love to hit the road and see different things along the way. It allows us time to talk and discuss what's on our minds and helps us clear our heads. When this pandemic is over, look out, road.

I am very much aware of what happens when you neglect your

free time. I get restless and moody. I tend to clam up and stop communicating, but when I do, it's usually to tell someone off.

The lessons in life should be easy enough to spot. The problem is that we tend to ignore them and wonder why life is so hard.

If you find yourself too far gone from taking care of your mental health, there are ways to get back on track. Start by taking little breaks just for yourself. Take fifteen minutes to just sit in your car or a room by yourself and meditate. Do that at least once a day for a while. Soon you will be thinking about a nice vacation, a getaway from the usual grind. Make plans to travel somewhere relaxing, then take that time and get yourself recharged.

I like to call this resting easy before I rest easy.

CHAPTER 5

It's a Dog's World

There's a saying that a dog can sense if a person is good or bad. I tend to believe that saying and often rely on Fido to sniff out the jerks in a crowd. I often wonder what goes on in the head of that guy as he stands there just looking at a dog barking uncontrollably at him.

I have hope that there will be a day when the scent of any living, breathing human being will not stave off the love of a dog. That fear is a distant memory, and we can live each day as if it were our last.

That said, I'm not sure that our faith in our favorite canine can be as bold toward a fowl such as a turkey. It has been a few years now, but there is a cemetery in the Kansas City area that was home to Tom the turkey. Tom would waddle up to a group of mourners at a graveside service, and he would squawk and gobble and sometimes peck at some of them. Most of the time, Tom was a comedic relief for the average mourner, but there were times when he would strike up the wrong pose, and his little skit became a burdensome interruption that got him in hot water with the cemetery staff. I often wonder whatever happened to old Tom as he just disappeared one day. No one seems to know, but legend has it that the last Thanksgiving Day feast at the cemetery garden house was a big hit.

Speaking of pets, according to memorialsblog.com, there are about 117 pet cemeteries in the United States officially. That does not include all the cats, dogs, and goldfish buried in my backyard.

I've worked with funeral directors who had to deal with families of presidents and movie stars. They all had a chance at life that most of us will never experience. But what we do have is so much more. We have a new chance to make our days the best days, to do what makes us happy. Sometimes that includes our favorite pet or even plant.

As I think about that sweet ninety-four-year-old lady from outside Kansas City, I can't help but wonder if all those plants and trees in her garden of love didn't know that she had moved on to another dimension. That the heavens opened their gates and welcomed her with open arms and then led her back to them in the form of rain and sunlight. I am certain that the one thing she never worried about was her funeral.

But she was an exception to the rule. In most cases, we are surrounded by people who love us, count on us, need to see us, and sometimes just think about us.

So as you move from one moment to another, stop worrying about tomorrow. Live the best moment you can right now. That's what our pets do. Have fun with it. Daydream. Bring others into your world, and let them see how blue the sky is or how beautiful the trees are. Smile and be smiled at. What would Fido do?

There's a story in the usnews.com about a dog named Cleo whose family had moved and taken him along from Olathe, Kansas, to their new home about fifty-seven miles away. Two years went by, and one day, Cleo came up missing. The family put out missing-dog signs and posted a Facebook announcement to see if anyone has seen their best friend. The people living in their old house in Olathe had housed Cleo after he made the long trek back to the homestead. After many attempts to locate the owner, they discovered the Facebook post, and Cleo was reunited with his family.

Now, Cleo was able to travel on foot for fifty-seven miles to find an old friend (his old house). If Cleo can make that trip on foot, we should be able to visit some old friends or relatives on four wheels. After all, most of us have driver's licenses. That's more than Cleo had.

A wise man once told me that if you don't like the way your day is going, you have all day to start over.

So be kind, and remember, the world you create today affects everyone around you. Make it a great one and connect with others.

I recall a time when we had to pick up the phone receiver and ask the operator to connect us to whoever we were calling. According to the way-back machine for me, that was in the fifties. We were careful not to make too many calls as we would be billed at the end of the month from Ma Bell, and long-distance calls could easily break the bank. So unless we conversed with neighbors, there was not a lot of communication too far away friends and relatives. There was the telegraph, or we would write letters every now and then and even include a picture if we were able to get the negatives to the drugstore in time. After all, it took weeks to get our pictures back, and most didn't turn out the way we hoped. Let's just say that we lived in a world without Photoshop.

Today, we have no excuse to skip a conversation unless you are just tired of listening to Aunt Martha. Let us count the ways:

1. House phone
2. Cell phone
3. E-mail
4. US mail
5. FEDEX, UPS, a million other common carriers
6. Facebook
7. Twitter
8. Instagram
9. Facetime
10. Instant messenger
11. Fax
12. Text message
13. Telepathy
14. Smoke signal

Okay, I get it. Faxing is way outdated, but you get the picture, right?

I recall a day when our supervisors tried to soften the blow as they introduced new technology to us with this little quip, "One day, there will be no need for paper as we embark on our new computer system and the World Wide Web." This always makes me think of that show, *The Office*.

Recently, my niece had to change communication with her son, who had joined the marines. She could write a letter and send it through the mail. No e-mails or text messages. No phone calls or Facetime. It must be like writing cursive after thirty years of typing.

Anyway, as you can see, we have no excuse to skip that conversation. There are just too many ways to communicate. So get in touch and stay in touch. A conversation, face-to-face, with a friend or family member is way better as the real deal than sending emojis over the airways.

If we prepared ourselves for that last day like we did for, say, Y2K or, as seismologists have done to get engineers on the right track designing buildings to withstand earthquakes at high magnitudes.

The Y2K fiasco was, by far, the most ridiculous stretch for fear we have ever been through. In case you are unfamiliar with Y2K, that was the term used for the calendar turning over from 1999 to 2000. Giving that event a title that read like an algebra problem was simply brilliant. People were told that there was a probability that at the strike of midnight on New Year's Day, the entire planet would go black because our computers were not tested to see what would happen when there would be no more 19--. Would they just stop operating at the strike of 2000? No one knew, and if they did, well, they didn't tell me. LOL.

People purchased hand-cranked radios and water filters like crazy. Nonperishable foods were flying off the shelves as well. It was insane and funny at the same time. I bet that that was the best year for celebrations. I wouldn't know; I was fast asleep before the ball dropped.

Well, as you know, nothing happened. Everything stayed on, and there were a lot of conspiracy speculations that this was a trick to get us off guard, that the real shutdown would occur in a few days, just when we are confident that everything is going to be okay.

Now, even though the Y2K thing was just a big letdown, people actually prepared for the worst. They believed that we would be ponding lumber with the Mennonites. Some even prepared fallout shelters with wood-burning stoves. The invention of solar couldn't come fast enough. Year 2005 was the year of solar. That is when people could actually have panels installed. Wow, just five years too late.

Even though that whole thing became a joke to many, merchandizers were pumping out Y2K shirts and hats and coffee mugs and beer mugs and just about anything that would accept the print. I'm pretty sure you can find a lot of these today at your local garage sale.

My point is this, we prepare for impending disasters like Y2K or earthquakes and hurricanes, and let's not forget tornadoes and floods. But we seem to take our final day much less serious. We live like we could live forever. I get that some of us just don't care. You are on your own island, and that is where you will stay until the end. But for the rest of us, we can start with understanding that everything we say and do affects others. But when we treat others like we want to be treated, it seems like the world just starts to blend better. And when that last day arrives, you will know that you were a huge part in bringing love and understanding to others.

A watered-down life is a life that just exists to get the day over. Don't be that person that just does enough to get by. When you wake up in the morning, you should have plans to make your day just a little bit better. I recall a young man that worked for me at one of the casket warehouses. He was a truck loader. Every time an expensive casket came along, he would make comments about how ridiculous it is to buy something so extravagant. He never thought of the body that would be rested inside that box. He almost seemed angry that a family would be viewing their loved one in this beautiful piece of art. One day, I asked him if he ever thought about his own funeral or even his last day. He barked back at me and said that he had never thought about it, but he would never think of spending the kind of money that it takes to be buried in a box this expensive. I said, "I'm guessing that the poor soul who's going to lie in this casket never thought about this either when he was your age. Don't judge people and you will not be judged." He said that he will probably just be cremated anyway. It's a lot cheaper. I responded, "I'll bet this poor old soul probably thought the same at your age."

In other words, you will probably change your mind a hundred times before that day arrives. So don't judge others. It took some time to get to the decision to be laid out in style like that.

Think about your pets for a moment. If they are like Cleo, they have heart. They have a love for what makes them safe and comfortable. When they hurt, they look for you to cure them. When they are hungry, they look for you to feed them. When they look for love, they look for you. They are perfect in every way when it comes to your relationship with them. They love you unconditionally and will lie by your side when you are in need. What they don't care about are your decisions on purchases. They don't care about your car or how big your house is. They don't judge.

Let's be like Cleo.

CHAPTER 6

Let Me Connect You

Now there's a concept. Connect with others. Our current environment seems more exclusive than inclusive. We seem to have lost the art of communicating with people who have other ideas. Rather they are political, religious, or even what sports team they root for. We have been raised to believe one thing while our neighbor was raised to believe another, but we still talk to our neighbor.

Standing in the middle of a cemetery one day as I was delivering a eulogy for a veteran of WWII, I noticed how different each headstone seemed. After the service, I wandered back to my car and stopped to read some of those markers. One gave a glowing send-off with a heart carved above the name. Another had a photo of the deceased and a poem that read, "Follow your path to the heavens and God will meet you there." There were old ones and new ones. But the one constant was the size of their graves. Not one living soul is so big in their stature that they take up more room in the graveyard than I. The pauper lies with the millionaire, the soldier and politician. If we can remember this, then maybe we can live that way too.

My mother used to tell me to respect my elders because one day, I would be one. As I grew older, I began to believe that respect is earned and should never be presented freely but accordingly. I learned to respect those who treat all as equal.

Living the life of happiness is being absent of negativity. Being absent of negativity means spreading your goodwill.

When you venture out into the world, you will be met with obstacles and hurdles. Not the least during a job interview. You will be asked to describe your best response to a difficult situation. You will be told that there is no wrong answer, that they just want to know your style before they make any hiring decisions. They will be correct. There are no wrong answers. If you want to follow a path of happiness, don't start out by lying on your job application. It will come back to bite you.

I recall giving an interview to a young man in Dallas a few years ago. He was applying to become a manager of a casket distribution center there. The district manager and I were holding the interviews together. Tag-teaming, if you will. He would ask a question then I would. It was designed to keep the interview moving and to give two perspectives on the applicant.

As my partner was asking some questions, I would be looking over the résumé to make sure we were not missing anything. As I glanced over the applicant's education history, I was surprised and wondered why no one caught this.

Right in the middle of the page, there it was, in full black-and-white print. We were interviewing a graduate of the Houston School of Clowns. And while I'm glancing at this golden piece of personal history, my interviewing partner had just asked, "What would you do if you found out one of your employees lied on their résumé?" He responded immediately with, "Well, I don't like being lied to so I would probably conduct a full investigation into why they lied and see if there was anything else that they lied about and then I would fire that person and make a full-on example of them." Keeping in mind that there are no wrong answers, watching him respond to the question with fury and fire, his face turned red and his eyes got dark and he puffed up like a cape rain frog when it got frightened.

I then asked what inspired him to attend clown school. My interviewing partner almost broke his neck as he turned to me with a "What the hell" look, as the applicant went into a tirade about an anger issue he had dealt with over the years. He explained that his counselor had suggested humor to relieve the pressure and help him calm down. Now, I don't remember the rest of that interview other than it was rather short, but I'm hoping that he found the job of his dreams down the road because I truly believe that honesty gets you what you are looking for.

I often think about what would have happened if that clown graduate had not put that on his résumé, and he had different responses to our inquiries and then we hired him to manage thirty people. Well, due to his honesty, that problem has been diverted. Hopefully, he picked up on our reactions and decided that his approach to life might need some tweaking.

My point to this rendering of the past is to let you know that moving down the road of life, you will be met with decisions. No one else can make them for you, but allow yourself to be guided by honesty and you will sleep better knowing you're in the right place. I guess the lesson here is to remember that one day, you will be eulogized by people with a perspective. You have choices in life, but none at your funeral.

The summer of 1959, I was seven years old. I was staying at my grandparents' house in Davenport, Iowa. They lived in an older bungalow on Grand Avenue in the northeast section of town. My grandma took me by the hand one day and said, "Come with me, Terry, we're going to a wake." Now, I was seven. I had no idea what a wake was, but I remembered my dad mentioning that one day when he took me fishing with him, so how bad could this be and why were we not taking fishing poles?

That day was like an adventure I can never forget. We walked to the corner of Grand Avenue and Central Park. There we boarded a bus. We rode that bus for a little while and then got off in downtown Davenport. Then we boarded another bus and rode it for a little while and then exited that bus somewhere in the burrows of the southwest end of Davenport. Now, from here we walked up this concrete staircase that had over a billion steps straight up. Once we reached the top of those stairs, we walked another 25 gazillion miles it seemed until we reached this house. As we approached the house, I saw a bunch of people walking up to the front porch and across the front of the house like they were in line at a buffet. Well, I was hungry from all that riding and walking so this was like light at the end of a dark tunnel. It was hot in the sun so when we got to the top stair of the porch, it felt like I just climbed Mount Everest and I was about to celebrate with some good food. As we shuffled down the path behind everyone else, I saw what was supposed to be a buffet. And then it hit me, there is this big casket sitting up on sawhorses. I could see the nose of a guy lying inside as I was too short to look all the way inside the casket. I held on to my grandma's hand and would not let go. I was frightened beyond belief.

In those days, you had the option of having the funeral at your own house. The funeral home folks would bring your loved one by and set him up for you wherever you wanted. Usually, that would be the front porch so the body didn't stink up the house. They would fill the casket with ice to keep the body from smelling, but that only helped a little.

Well, my appetite disappeared as I waited for all the condolences to get over so we could get out of there. I remember that I was kind of pissed at my grandmother for doing that to me. On the way home, she explained who her friend was and that she just wanted to make damn sure he was dead and brought me along to keep her from spitting on the body. I didn't know what to say so I just said, "You're welcome."

We laughed all the way home.

That was my first encounter with the death industry. From there, it seemed that nothing shocked me. I didn't know at the time, but in some way, I was prepared from then on for anything.

When death knocked on the door of a friend or family, I was ready to see it differently. I could comfort more and shriek less although it would be a good ten years before that had to happen. That is when my grandfather passed away. We watched him slip further and further into dementia until he finally met his maker. Because of the trauma of watching him suffer, his death was more of a blessing to him and us.

I watched my grandma die while holding her hand when she was suffering from a cancer lump to her throat. She was always the bright spot in my life growing up. She always made me smile. That was a day that I'll never forget. My poor grandma was the victim of a shyster that sold her house out from under her. That's a story all by itself and will have to be told in another book. Anyway, she had to move to an apartment in downtown Davenport. One day she was walking to the store and slipped on ice as she was walking across the street. A car was making a right-hand turn and drove over her. She sustained some broken bones, but what really messed her up was a pocket of cancer that had formed in her neck. When she was in the hospital for her injuries, that pocket turned into a monster and started eating her up. That was a tough one for myself and everyone else in the family. Anyway, as I watched her take her last breath, all I could think of was all the good times I had with her at her house on Grand Avenue.

I was there when my mother passed, and I was the first one on the scene after my dad had left us. Each time, it seemed to me that there was a lesson in their death. Each time, I would ask myself where I go from here, and each time the path just lit up and reserved my spot on the next journey. It has always been a connection to the next dimension. For whatever reason, I felt a sense of relief that I was free to move on and see what life has for me in the next block of time.

Sometimes death can rip a family apart. Don't let that happen in your family. Don't look at animent possessions as anything other than that. Let it go. That goes for money as well. Trust me, it will destroy your family if you let it.

So as you find yourself disconnected through the loss of a loved one, allow yourself the glory of connecting to the next chapter in your life. My aunt Pink would say, "Think of the possibilities of your future. There's no limit. Now move along."

Here lies a teller, a song he sings no more
He rest upon the willow tree
and sleeps so tenderly

My love for life will bring him back
I swear to you that's true
Just give me his hand and his love for the land
and I'll give him the sky so blue

Here lies a teller, God's gift to you and I
He fades into the world of green
and soon our last goodbye

Here lies a teller, his smiles that brought us joy
it's not about his leaving now
the future now seems coy

Here lies the teller
don't wait for eyes to dry

Here lies the teller
It's time to say goodbye. (TK White)

CHAPTER 7

Strap Me to a Pole

Another aspect of the death-care industry that often escapes the layman's perception of preparedness is the timing of decision making.

Now, I'm not going to pretend that "funeral planning" isn't boring. It is. And we all know it. When you are young and active, the last thing you want to talk about is your funeral, unless it's with your buddies. We've all had that discussion about how we want to go out. Here's some that I have encountered from some pals:

- Shoot me out of a canon.
- Put ice and beer in my casket.
- Strap me to a pole and set me on fire.
- Drop me out of a plane.
- Cremate me and put my ashes in someone's brownies.
- Take me to a taxidermist.
- Bury me facedown so you can all kiss my ass goodbye.
- Put popcorn in my pockets then cremate me.
- Tie me to my motorcycle and let me down easy.
- Fill me with those little booze bottles and make a piñata out of me.
- Cover me in lacquer and make me into a mannequin.
- Use me as a doorstop.
- Tie me to a post and put me in the cornfield as a scarecrow.
- Tie my hands to a shopping cart, put a blue vest on me, and set me up as a Walmart greeter.
- Wrap me up in burlap and drop me off at the Goodwill.
- I don't care what you do to me, just don't scratch my car.

And the list goes on.

I recall the request of a deceased when I was working in Southern California, that a phone be placed in her casket, just in case she is brought back to life and needs to have a conversation.

There's no end to the rational or lack of rational thinking during the process of arranging a funeral. If you have ever been involved with a soon-to-be bride arranging her wedding, then you must know that there are also unlimited crazies that happen during the arrangement of your own funeral.

We all like to think that our pageant into the sky will be different than any we have seen. Truth is, you won't get to see it. My advice is to make every day a pageant of your dreams. That way, you can enjoy them with your family and friends.

Woody Guthrie wrote a song called "Hobo's Lullaby." The song reminds us all to do what makes you happy, regardless of what others may think. Listening to this song, I imagine a life on the road, riding the rails, free as free can be. I think about how a person can do this and survive and then wonder what my life would be like doing just that. No responsibilities, just the wind in my hair and the sun in my eyes.

The takeaway is as we keep moving forward, every moment and every curve, take in all the experiences you can. Today, you are a train conductor, tomorrow you may be a hobo traveling on the same train. Either way, you end up at the same location. Some like to call that heaven.

As I sit and write what's on my mind, I can't help but wonder what it would be like to be stifled in thoughts. What is it like where expression is frowned upon? I thank God for the freedom to offer these pages, as the death-care industry is not for the timid. It is, however, important to be familiar with certain aspects of this world. Life is hard enough without going into a moment of loss blindfolded and vulnerable to misinformation. But I also want you to know that there are bright spots to celebrate as well.

Pain and suffering has a price, monetary as well as psychologically. There are people who like to keep to themselves and hunker down in their dens as the rest of the world is in constant connective mode. Most of us like to keep up with each other. We like to hang out with our friends and are constantly hovering over social media to see what the word of the day is.

At this writing, we are in the midst of a pandemic known as COVID-19. Doctors and scientists are asking us to hunker down in our homes and wear masks when we do go out. I have a friend who always has kept to himself. He is shy and hates going out to dinner or anywhere else. He told me the other day that this is just his cup of tea and if I needed any pointers on self-quarantine to let him know. When this is over, I'm going to start spending more time with those that I miss. I have family and friends all over the country, and I have to admit, I am one of those people who kept saying, someday I'm road tripping and going on some serious visits. But until then, I'm hanging around picking up these crazy ideas from friends around the world.

When the baby boomers started to become senior citizens (age sixty-two) in 2008, it was expected that the death rate would start to skyrocket. But what actually happened was a mixed bag of events. First, the cremation rate started to increase, and the death rate stayed pretty flat at the time. A lot can be said for modern medicine and the influx of taking care of ourselves that became a trend. Eating well and exercising was the thrill of the times for boomers over the years. Those numbers did increase eventually, but not at the rate that was expected. Yay, baby boomers.

What is amazing is the uptick in science and technology and the engagement of new ideas with lifesaving procedures that were not even a dream a mere ten to twenty years earlier. Think of the improvements with heart transplants and reversal of cancer cells just to name a couple.

Anyway, it's great to know that our mortality rate has improved and that we will probably hang with each other a little while longer. But don't wait too long. Anything could happen, and I don't mean just natural causes. COVID-19 is teaching us that now.

There was a time when the funeral was laid out in such a way that we expected certain arrangements to take place. After all, that's just the way things have always been done. The casket sits in the middle of the chapel, and the flowers are set up all around, and the preacher reads some prayers, and then we head to the cemetery and lower Uncle Bob down into this hole. And then there's food.

In the late 1900s and early 2000s, the funeral industry started making some serious changes.

Funeral home owners began to realize that changes needed to be made. The "new" family mouthpiece is younger and has different views on this celebration of death. For one, they don't like that a normal funeral has to cost an arm and a leg. They lean toward a less-expensive route to heaven. This was the new dawn of cremation growth.

Cremation was cheaper, and a service could be held at the family farm or golf club. There is no need for all this expensive casket and use of the funeral home personnel and chapel.

The Catholic church was cool with cremation, but there were rules. They could bury, but not scatter. Well, back to the funeral home we go, and let's talk about a grave opening and closing.

In the early 2000s, the cost of a single grave with a headstone and opening and closing was around $2,000, give or take a $1,000, depending on the area of the country you lay your loved one.

So some got the idea that scattering Dad's ashes all over the lake he loved to fish in was a much better idea. I mean, how appropriate is that. Everyone would agree that Dad would be happy as fish food. That is, until the ranger catches them littering. As it turns out, it has become difficult to find a place to unload the cremated remains of the guy that taught you how to ride a bike. Now, for a long time, people thought that the ashes of your loved one had some sort of damaging effect on the environment; and if we inhaled any of it, we could get infected with God knows what. The truth is, cremated remains are an excellent fertilizer for mother earth but are not harmful if inhaled unless, of course, you snorted Dad like cocaine.

Another invention that came our way was the ash press, as I call it. You can now have cousin Dave's ashes pressed into a diamond and mounted on a ring. And if Dave had a lousy disposition at times, you could call it your mood ring.

You can also divide the ashes up amongst your siblings and grandkids and have small amounts put into little lockets for necklaces or bracelets. The possibilities are endless.

So you have options. You are not saddled with a run-of-the-mill funeral. But that doesn't mean that you cannot go that direction. Casket companies are offering up caskets that have interchangeable corners and statues for the head dish and drawers in the foot dish and of course the old standby panel that fits into the head dish to give your loved one a sense of holiness, with sayings like "Going home" or "In God's hands now."

The funeral is a personal tribute to a loved one. It is a time for reflection and to gather with those who can comfort the ones left behind. If there are hard feelings between family members, it is the one time to put your difference aside. Whatever you are left with, it will never be enough to fill the void. That is what a funeral is for. It is for people to come and help fill that void, if only for an hour or two.

The trend toward cremation and then a small immediate family memorial sometime down the road, in my opinion, is disrespectful. I understand the cost factor, but if you let your local funeral home help you, they can give you the service that your loved one and you deserve.

While there are options for every lifestyle while we are still on the top side of the sod, there should be for that send-off to the heavens as well. And there are. I will highlight some of those in chapter 10.

Keep in mind that families today are spread all over the country. In the old days, most everybody still lived in the town that you grew up in. You got a job at the local foundry and raised your family down the street from where you grew up. Everyone knew everyone, and the world was an easier place to be.

But then modern technology started ruining things for the family unit. They made it easier to travel, and big corporations were shipping personnel all over the damn place. Our fathers worked at the same place all their lives while we moved from job to job like we're delivering pizzas or something.

So life is different now than it used to be. In most cases, the funeral professional is privy to all that and is equipped to deal with those changes. Many times, funerals are delayed because brother Tom is coming in from out of town and can't make the original service on time.

If only things stayed the same. Most of us would rather they did, but they don't. Listen to your younger children. Let them help you through all the gridlock turnstiles, and you will be thankful that you did.

CHAPTER 8

Let Go

A Ride for Charlie

Reliving the past in a dark limousine.
A family talks quietly about the grave they will see.
They summon some memories and laugh a bit too.
They cry as they bring all the best of his days.
To the image of Charlie and all that he was.
It's just about over, as the hearse makes a pause.
I guess this is it, says the lady in black.
Thank you for the ride sir, said the man in the back.
The rain kept it's distance as they marched to the grave.
And there was our Charlie, we just couldn't save. (TK White)

As a death-care professional, there are times that are less desirable than others.

A few years ago, I was part of a group of funeral folks attending a disinterment (that is when a deceased is exhumed from the grave). This particular disinterment was performed so that the family of the deceased can move her to a cemetery closer to their home. Location, location, location.

There are many reasons to perform a grave-digging ceremony

like this. In most cases, they are to gather more evidence regarding a murder, but sometimes it's just for a reunion.

The key to a happy life is to focus on *your* happiness. To do the things that make you happy. One can only hope that we can all let go of those who went before us so that we can enjoy what is left.

Now, I'm not suggesting that you try to forget all the good times and wonderful experiences you had with your loved ones. That would be unmanageable. What I am suggesting is that you see to it that time is spent enjoying those that are still breathing, including yourself.

Amit Ray wrote,

If you want to fly in the sky, you need to leave the earth.
If you want to move forward, you need to let go the past
that drags you down.

Most of us have found ourselves stuck in a rut of frustrating confinement. We are sold on an idea that struck us when we are vulnerable because of our dislikes or hatred toward an idea or a representation of something that disagrees with our core beliefs.

We recoil from reasonable debate and hide in our cocoon of fear, refusing any reason toward reality. And then we wonder where all our friends disappeared to. We believe that we are not alone in our convictions until we are alone at last.

Don't let this happen to you if you can avoid it. We have become a divided world. We have allowed our fears to take over and control our decision making.

We stop rationalizing and start to build walls around us, where no new ideas or compassion can penetrate. We look at the world as evil and less trusting than what we have wrapped ourselves in.

We look for proof of our convictions instead of reasons from other ideas.

If we could look at our fellow humans and try to understand their ideas and convictions, then we will start to unravel the coil of hate that has gripped our world. What draws one to a belief? Why are they so passionate about what they believe? Is there any concrete evidence to present to them that would direct them to a different path? If the answer to that last one is no, then applaud them for their conventions and move on.

Let it go. If we can just accept the fact that we all believe in different ways and for different reasons, then, and only then, will we be able to accept each other as fellow human beings.

Not too long ago, I was following a conversation on Facebook regarding "best pizza in town." The conversation started out okay, but it wasn't too far down the page before the name-calling started. I was amazed at how quickly things escalated. Remember that the whole discussion was about pizza. Knowing that everyone has different taste buds and tolerance for smell, I could not believe that there would be such dissent for someone's inherited genes for the taste of pepperoni.

If we can become rabid over differing taste buds, how in the world could we handle another's taste for liberty or freedom, our rights to be safe, or even the side of the tracks we are from?

When people praise the Lord on Sunday and then call for genocide on Monday toward a group of people just because of what side of an imaginary line they were born on, that calls for a reevaluation of the core of our souls. Every living, breathing human being has a right to be on earth. Where on earth is a choice that belongs to the individual. I am glad to have you as neighbors.

I suggest that we all take a hint from Epictetus: "Is freedom anything else than the right to live as we wish? Nothing else."

So let it go. Refresh your mind with the idea that we are all free to live the life we love as long as it does not interfere with others and with the people we love and in the land we love. Remember that you will have a "Last Day." You will have a final chapter and a last sentence to mark the conclusion of your journey. Do you really think that your opinion about where someone else should live is relevant to your spot in the cemetery? Keep your thoughts positive. Step away from the spiked gears of politics or whose religion is the bomb. You'll be happier for that.

Keep a journal of all the things that happened throughout your life. And even some of the bad ones as well. Remember that every episode of your life made you who you are.

I encourage everyone to seek out someone whom you can count on to finish out your wishes for that day of celebration. Remember that as you stumble through life, there will be people that come and go. You need to have a plan that can be executed in the event that you leave this world and your loved ones are totally lost about what to do and who to call for help. So while you're still of sound mind, get to know your local funeral professional. Let them know how you want to be remembered on that day that you will have no control over then.

There was a time when families used the same funeral home for generations. Our world has changed so much that people don't stay where they grew up anymore. Companies transfer people like birds migrate anywhere. Professionals don't stay at one company like they did in the years leading up to the 1980s. It has become easier to move about the country or even the world so we tend to not stay put for long.

Because of this transformation in mobility, the funeral business has been forced to comply with these changing lifestyles. Most, if not all by now, funeral professionals are prepared to work with you as you plan your last day. They understand that there is that chance that you might be living in Mytown USA instead of Yourtown USA when your last breath is exhaled. They have plans for that, plans that can transfer to another funeral home in another town. So don't let that thought of "Where will I be" get in the way of doing the right thing.

To the Funeral Professional

Here's to you.

It is up to you to make yourselves known. I suggest you join your local chapters of business pros, chambers, or church groups. Let everyone see you and know you. Many of you already do this. Let them know that you are available to help them.

I don't want to have plumbing issues. But I will one day, and when that day comes, I'll have to pay a plumber. Wouldn't it be nice if I had the assurance that there is someone I can call and count on to alleviate me of the burden?

Get out there and let them know that they can enjoy life without the concerns for the afterlife. I get that some will seem selfish and lack the forethought of what that pageant to the sky should look like or even who will pay for it. But you know the drill, "The only certain in life is death and taxes," and I'm guessing that most of you are not accountants.

So be that guy/gal that we refer to when we say, "I have a guy/gal."

I'll Just Donate My Body

I hope you will take this seriously soon. Before it is too late. By the way, for those who claim that you are just going to donate your body to science, I suggest you get with a med school or organization that will facilitate your wishes. Otherwise, you will be leaving your family with a huge burden because there is paperwork and signatures needed in order to have that legally processed. In other words, that little heart thing on your license looks cool and all, but you need to talk to the right people and get your spouse to agree with a signature.

Here are some websites that an help. I got these from Google"

HYPERLINK
"https://www.googleadservices.com/pagead/aclk?sa=L&ai=DChcS
Ewix_ve0xtDqAhXIRdUKHQ8qA2cYABABGgJpbQ&ohost=
www.google.com&cid=CAESQOD2KlgfbrD9BVoHJv-xuy-TKlG
Kd7ucMrh_epB9ZvB3DjoNO58wqqSi24TYXzTOqASqdVTbDfa
40Mk2fYuMZ48&sig=AOD64_0pkDZRNdDm1vhQgkyiAu_
HJRT6Ig&q=&ved=2ahUKEwjllu60xtDqAhWKB80KHcDhCO
4Q0Qx6BAgPEAE&adurl=" www.genesislegacy.org/

HYPERLINK
"https://www.googleadservices.com/pagead/aclk?sa=L&ai=DChcS

Ewix_ve0xtDqAhXIRdUKHQ8qA2cYABAAGgJpbQ&ohost=
www.google.com&cid=CAESQOD2KlgfbrD9BVoHJv-xuy-TKlG
Kd7ucMrh_epB9ZvB3DjoNO58wqqSi24TYXzTOqASqdVTbDf
a40Mk2fYuMZ48&sig=AOD64_21aG1wwj4u7yk9PPoJtoMJp0C
V8Q&q=&ved=2ahUKEwjllu60xtDqAhWKB80KHcDhCO4Q0
Qx6BAgOEAE&adurl=" www.unitedtissue.org/
HYPERLINK
"https://www.sciencecare.com/how-does-the-body-donation-process-work"
www.sciencecare.com

These might get you started. You can also contact your favorite medical school or your local funeral director. There is no short supply of takers, but you really need to do your homework.

CHAPTER 9

CDC

CDC Reveals Teenage Suicide Has Increased 76 Percent in Last Decade

Why do we continue to let this happen? I'm reminded of the fisherman that discovered dead bodies floating down the river. After reporting his findings to the authorities and watching them scratch their heads, he suggested that they look upstream to see where the flow began.

Some argue that the problem is due to when parents start allowing things like TV and video games to become the new babysitters. I believe that the mind is much more complicated than that.

To conclude what might have happened, what path was taken to bring someone to the brink of suicide takes paying attention and acting on cue. But it is still not that simple. We have learned over time that many victims of suicide never let on that there is anything wrong.

We have all had that friend or family member who seemed to struggle with life. If you are like me, you probably wondered how they can be so down when you are so up. It is true that there are chemical imbalance concepts that most of us are not equipped to deal with. But we are equipped with a brain, and this is a good time to use it. There are people who can work with the clinically depressed. A good question is to ask if they are seeing anyone who can help them.

Never let your fears interfere with action. Be prepared to approach a friend or family member who seems to be struggling. In most cases, all you need to do is just sit and listen. I am guilty as anyone when that moment strikes. It is easy to take the easy route and just move along and pretend that nothing is wrong. The world needs more of us to stop and lend an ear every now and then. Just imagine if you were in a place of despair and no one cared. Let's be better at this. All it can do is help.

When a family visits a funeral home to make arrangements for their loved one, they are already stricken with sorrow and pain. They fear the future without the presence of them. Their world had been turned upside down. It is at this time that they need the understanding and compassion of others. But when they are grieving the loss of a child or any loved one from suicide, it changes their world in ways that pierces their hearts for years to come. If you have never experienced the loss of a loved one from suicide, you can never know the true pain it leaves for those left behind.

The key to comfort is listening. The path to healing is communication. Protect your heart by giving of it, and you shall bring joy to those who inhale and breathe your love. When you feel a breeze on your face, think of the love of others.

Many years ago, as a young teenager, I worked the night shift in a commercial bakery. There were just the two of us on that shift, an older guy named Henry and me. We made fruitcakes. That was all we made—fruitcakes. To this day, I can't stand the sight or smell of fruitcake. But what I miss about those nights was the constant ramblings of that old guy Henry. He would talk about his love life like he was Pablo of the Quad Cities. I would let him ramble on because it made him happy and it made the night go by faster. One story that sticks out in my memories is the night Henry was walking one of his lovely ladies home when he was confronted by another one. As he described the encounter, there was quite a discomfort of jealousy between the two ladies, but before the night had ended, he described a stroll down the street with both, one on each arm.

I was young and very impressionable, so I was a great audience for Henry. Every now and then, as our shift ended, he would ask me to peek outside and describe the car waiting for him. That would let him know which lady was picking him up. I knew he just wanted to impress me. I remember that each time, there would be a different car waiting. To me, that was a good visual of his love life.

Now you're probably thinking that eventually, I discovered that Henry was a good storyteller but liked to embellish to a large degree. I was never able to verify his stories, not because I tried and failed, but because I didn't want to know if they were false. I liked Henry just the way he was. I wanted to believe that he was the Fabio of the Quad Cities. After all, what does that hurt? It made me happy to see Henry gleam with pride as he spoke, and it seemed to make him happy to have someone to tell these stories to.

I know that there are people in all of our lives that like to tell stories of the past. What a great world this would be if we stopped being so busy and let ourselves become immersed into their lives. Let them speak of the past. Let them paint a picture of fantasy or of a world left behind. It can bring joy to you and open your eyes to the unknown. It could even help you understand the world around you. The more you know, the closer you become. Sometimes that is the key to helping those who need a bended ear and could save a life.

Getting back to the CDC, at this writing, there have been over 135,000 people die from COVID-19 in the United States. We have seen videos of mass graves. People had to die alone. No one is allowed in hospital rooms unless you are sick or a medical staffer.

Businesses are closing down and unemployment is at an all-new high reaching, 13–16 percent. Schools closed early, and graduations have been canceled. And it seems everyone has gone completely mad.

There is always a silver lining to every disaster. People are spending more time with family. Less time is being spent rushing around, gathering up airline tickets and hotel reservations.

Parents are learning how to teach their own children, and some are even getting to know their kids. More people are working from home instead of cluttering up our roadways.

Of course, there are bad fallouts from this virus as well, not the least the idea of needing mass graves, but for the purpose of this book, I'd like to focus on the good.

By now, most people have known at least one person who had been diagnosed with the virus. So it's a pretty good chance that most people have had thoughts of losing a loved one or even their own life from this pandemic. I know that I have. I have asked myself if I would be ready or if my family would be okay without me. Lawyers have seen a huge spike in people getting their affairs in order from April to June 2020.

My true hope is that we survive and learn from this. That family is precious, and our lives are too delicate to take for granted.

My heart goes out to those who lost a loved one and especially to those who did not get to say goodbye because no one is allowed into an ER or a hospital room other than the patient and medical staff. When this is all over, there will be people all over, needing to talk it out with someone. Families are being torn apart and left with nothing, not even a gathering that could help ease the pain. For sure, there are some celebrations occurring here and there, but those seem to contract more viruses and then it starts all over.

This COVID-19 pandemic will be a subject for another or many books to come, but for now, let's show each other that we are strong for each other and work through the fog.

CHAPTER 10

Bad Religion

I do not believe in the practice of pageantry in order to save my soul. I do believe in a faith-based way of living though. Having faith in myself means that I have chosen to believe in my ability to survive whatever is tossed my way. It helps me to trust that there is a spirit within me guiding me along the way.

It also helps that I believe in the Golden Rule; "Treat others as you wish to be treated" is not a hard concept to engage in. It does, however, get lost in the pebbles of life if you can imagine each of our emotions being represented as a pebble.

One of the great things about not being tied down to a certain religious faith is that you can pick and choose what part of the Bible fits your needs.

Seriously though, we all know people of different faiths who seem a little offbeat. Some let their beliefs get in the way of someone else's beliefs. I'm sure you are all familiar with the baker and the gay couple. Well, as it turns out, the baker's religion tells him that he must not support gay weddings. And the gay couple believes that the baker must put his beliefs aside so that they can have cake. What should have happened is this: The baker explains to the gay couple that his hands are tied because he's too closed minded to make decisions without the guidance of some half-baked (no pun intended), made-up biblical rule that's roughly 2,700 years old and has been reinterpreted as many times in as many languages.

The rule we refer to is this: "Therefore a man shall leave his father and his mother and hold fast to his wife, and the two shall become one flesh" (Matt. 19:5).

This is the one that started all the others, and then it just mushroomed into this crazy encyclopedia of thousands of different interpretations of the word of God. Truth is, nothing in the Bible is the word of God. It is all the word of prophets and stagehands that had some real cool ideas and started telling everybody that "this is what God told me to tell you." Don't get me wrong, there are some great teachings in the Bible, like the following:

> *Let love be without hypocrisy. Abhor what is evil; cling to what is good.* (Rom. 12:9, NASB)

I am in awe of people who attend church, stick to their beliefs, and practice what they preach. I follow those who respect others for their ideas and understanding. If we all had the same ideas, there would be no progress. So keep it classy and let others have their day their way. That's part of feeling the love.

We get mad, upset, hurt, disappointed, envious, and even anxious. And that's just while driving to the store. The day is filled with ups and downs. There is no way every day will be perfect. However, there are ways to help make your day better, and that is how you treat others.

I have a friend who spends most of her free time feeding and clothing the homeless folks in Kansas City. She never brags about her work and makes it abundantly clear that she does not want to be celebrated for what she does. In my eyes, she is more godly than anyone walking out of Sunday worship service.

There's a lot to be said for the human race. Some of us are grateful, caring, and giving; others are suspicious, greedy, and needy.

During my experience in the distribution part of the death-care years, I managed casket warehouses throughout the country. This took me to places like Chicago; Milwaukee; Green Bay; Kansas City; Wichita, Kansas; Fullerton, California; San Diego, California; Sacramento, California; Las Vegas, Nevada; Houston, Texas; and other locations. I was challenged with supervising employees in all these locations.

One of the things that I learned over these years was that everyone has a style of living, of survival, of dealing with everything that comes their way. We are all taught at an early age how to respond to any situation by watching our elders. As we age and develop our own mechanisms for survival, we tend to drag some of what we grew up with along for the ride.

Sometimes that's good and sometimes not so much. But the best part of this job was the experience of meeting and enjoying so many people from so many different parts of the country. The one thing I have learned is that people are good and bad all over the place. I wish I had been a psychology major to help sort all of them out.

Back in the nineties, I had an employee working under me as "customer service representative." His job was to deliver caskets to funeral homes. He was expected to make sure each casket delivered was damage-free and clean. I had received a number of complaints about him from funeral professionals, claiming that he never checked for damage or cleaned caskets before leaving them. I had confronted him a number of times about this, and it seemed to go in one ear and out the other. Knowing that he had a family to feed and house, I looked for ways to get him to improve instead of reacting with a pink slip, but it was beginning to seem that he would not take my warnings. So I decided to ride along with him and get to know him. Maybe this would give me some insights on how to help him improve.

After a very long day of uncomfortable conversations and introductions to funeral home representatives, I surmised that my friend had personal issues he had been dealing with. Without going into great detail, let's just say his mind was not in his work. Once he started unloading his cancerous swill that was eating up his daily life, he didn't stop. The rest of the day was filled with him talking and me listening.

As the days went by, I would monitor my new friend each morning and at the end of the day. What had once seemed a defiant, hard-to-reach employee became a letter-perfect example of how to get the job done right.

Recognizing an underlying issue that will derail progress is progress. Without realizing what was happening just by keeping my mouth shut and listening, before my eyes, I was allowing my friend to unload all his poison so that he may live again.

I like to believe that the Golden Rule played a huge part in mending a life that was on the brink of destruction. Had I just thought for myself and refused to listen to his troubles, who knows how deep he could have fallen?

It's important to always remember that each and every one of us comes as a packaged deal. We have family, relationships, bills, and other obligations that keep our minds occupied. The Golden Rule says that we should treat others as we would like to be treated. So before you judge someone, ask yourself how you would want to be treated. In most cases, it's just as simple as listening.

I'm not going to pretend that I have all the answers. Hell, I don't even have a copy of the manual for this thing called life. I'm just winging it like the rest of you. But I know how I feel when I am around you. That's why I like being around you. You know who you are.

It is important to remember that all religions have a platform to present their ideas. They all use the Golden Rule as that platform. The wording will be different, but the idea is the same. There are countless religious faiths, and they all have a path to heaven. Some are through rituals, and some are through man-made beliefs, like the absence of pork or how you bury your dead and the wearing of a burka. Let's not forget that the Catholic faith will have you profess your sins to a priest and then offer up a shot of wine at 10:00 a.m. mass. I have attended Jewish funerals where they needed to get Elijah in the ground before the sun goes down. Oh, and let's not forget that the casket cannot have any metal in it at all. There are thousands of different faiths throughout the world and as many paths to the castle in the sky, but they all start out and follow the simple idea of the Golden Rule.

I have never figured out the rationale for certain faiths to disown a member of their club because they married outside of the church. Of course, that doesn't seem to be as big an issue today as it once was. That's progress, I guess.

If we are all God's children, then why do we have to be separated into tribes? I believe that if our forefathers had just mixed it up more, by now we would all be the same religion and color. There would be no reason for doubt. We would not know borders and would hopefully see each other as humans and not members of different tribes. I know I'm starting to sound like a John Lennon song, but think of the progress we could make if we just learned to work with each other and share ideas instead of ethnic jokes.

I blame religion for a lot of our troubles today. There are people in this world who believe that they have let their religion down, and that leads to the destruction of the mind. They feel that they need to hide from society, and they are constantly doubting everything they do and think. No one should ever feel that they are less of a person than anyone else. Let's not ever forget that.

And that, my friends, is the path of the Golden Rule.

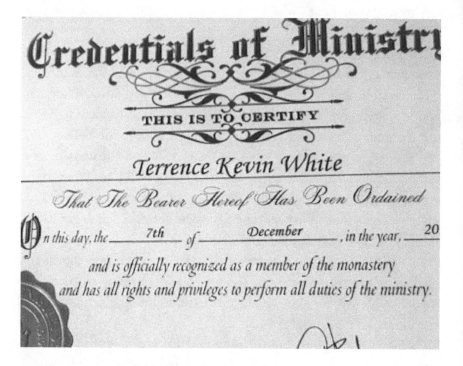

Besides the offering of eulogies for the loved ones in need, over time, I have performed a number of weddings. Most were for close friends, but there were others that presented themselves to me as friends of friends and even some that found my name on a card at another ceremony. *I'm just glad it wasn't a bathroom at a gas station.* This is another path that allowed me the pleasure of meeting some interesting people through the years. The soon-to-be bride is no exception and can sometimes be described as a distinction of royalty.

I have yet to be part of a wedding ceremony that wasn't planned by the bride in totality. Oh, every now and then the groom will try to take credit for part of the festivities, but it is not long before he is completely cured of any idea that he had a hand in any of it.

Weddings are another form of celebration. It's the beginning of a new partnership. Most of the weddings that I presided over were pageants for the bride and groom and a bridge from what once was to what will be. If these weddings of today are any indication of the future funerals, well, there won't be much in the line of a religious celebration. Not that they had no religious upbringing or held on to a faith of choice, it has been more that they have drifted away from the traditional holy consecration of their respective faiths.

I always ask the couple about their faith and if they would like references to that in their ceremony. The answers that I get are mixed. Some prefer to have references, such as prayers and traditional pageant, and some prefer not to include anything but special wordings; that means that they sometimes write their own vows. Interestingly, a lot of the couples that opt in on a faith-based ceremony want to please Mom or Aunt Betty who will be attending and are already disappointed that the wedding is not being held at Our Lady of the Most High and their nuptials are not offered to them by its pastor.

Now, there's a lot to be said for holding your allegiance to a certain faith. Mom and Aunt Betty have a treasure chest full of reasons why they feel this way. Their faith got them this far in life. Who are we to argue with that kind of success? My offerings are to those who have a need to follow their hearts even if it's along a different path.

For various reasons, folks have wandered away from their religion. It is not up to me or anyone else to question their reasons. What I have found is that most still hang on to their faith. They still believe in the doctrine of that faith. They just don't understand why there is a celebrated ritual that needs to be witnessed on a weekly schedule.

Without getting into statistics, it seems that the younger the generation, the farther they are from the brick-and-mortar church.

I hope that you can all find a faith to believe in. Even if it's that spirit from within, I highly recommend that if you are looking for that special piece of serenity, remember where it all starts: the Golden Rule.

Keep in mind that even within each religious faith, there are as many variations of its doctrine as there are heads filling the pews. If you think about the thousands of rewrites of the Bible and as many interpretations of each, you can understand why a baker thinks he is instructed to reject a gay couple or why it took the Catholic church so long to accept cremation. When my lovely bride Mary and I decided to get married, we were rejected by the Catholic church because we were once married to someone else. So we got married in a Lutheran church. Now, if you have ever been to a service at a Catholic church and a Lutheran church, then you know that there is hardly any difference. They are both of the Christian faith, and both hold the same rituals every Sunday. Martin Luther, a Protestant, tried to reform the Catholic church until the pope kicked him out, so then he started his own Lutheran church way back in the 1500s.

So if your heart is telling you to tie the knot, don't let rituals get in your way. I am very fortunate that I have been a part of so many lives that decided to reach for a new journey with someone they love. Let's keep an open mind and let the lovefest take place.

The average age at death in the United States is seventy-nine, and the average age of couples getting married is around twenty-seven. That means that a couple could live as one for fifty-two years. That is over half a century of love if you can keep it together. Think about that journey. There will be children and grandkids. There will be heartbreak and laughter. Jobs will come and go. Houses to move in and out of. Neighbors to keep in touch with. Cars that will need to be traded after Junior destroys your favorite Impala. Boyfriends, girlfriends. Dogs, cats, lost hamsters, and found turtles. There will be fishing trips and camping. Prom dates and football games. Trust me, you're not getting to the end of this life without some scratches. But every moment will be a step toward the end. Have faith and fun at the same time.

The Bible says in John 2:18, "There is no fear in love, but perfect love drives out fear."

If we continue to focus on the idea of love, then we can destroy fear and hate. It's that simple. That moment when we have to say goodbye is the hardest moment in life. When we leave our children at the curb in front of their dorm, when we put Mom or Dad in a nursing home, when we hug our kids because you're moving to another state or they are, when you break up or get divorced, it's all just practice for that last day. If you are lucky enough to say goodbye, it still hurts; but with all the love you have for your loved one, the one thing you fear is life without them.

I want to go back to our friend who lay alone in her casket at the cemetery and then only four people showed up to say goodbye. Chances are that there was no one at her bedside when the proper time arrived to say goodbye. Family was too busy. Doctors, lawyers, accountants, they were all too busy to spend a few minutes to say goodbye. She left without a care in the world. Her casket was beautiful as she lay with no flowers by her side. No one mourned her death. As I stood by her casket, I bowed my head. I asked the good Lord to receive her and comfort her. I asked that she return to earth as rain and sun to comfort her garden. I asked that her garden accept her glory in that form and to forgive those who forgot her. I prayed the Lord's Prayer and asked that he directs his loving hand to those in distress and those who lost their way. I gave her a eulogy that was deserving to the least of us and the best of us.

This day was hard. It was the hardest service to give. I know that she had family and friends. Where were they? The funeral director was kind and loving to the four people as she directed them toward the casket. The day was hot, but I could not feel the heat. The trees were waving with their branches.

CHAPTER 11

Losing a Friend and the Bottle

*If you live to be 100, I hope I live to be 100 minus 1 day,
so I never have to live without you.*

—Winnie the Pooh

The summer of 1998, my family and I moved to Lee's Summit, Missouri. My company had promoted me and moved us there from Milwaukee, Wisconsin.

There was something in the air in this center of the world. Lee's Summit is a southeastern suburb of Kansas City. Like most metropolises, all the burbs kind of ran together so you aren't sure where one starts and the other stops. But what was different about this metropolis was the air of friendship everywhere we went rather that was at the grocery store, gas station, city hall, or just out walking. Everyone had a friendly greeting. Eventually, this would rub off. I started feeling more positive about everything. It became easier to approach others and less fear of rejection or even retaliation. Not that I ever feared much about either, but I think everyone has a certain amount of fear that hides beneath the surface.

Our new neighbors were visibly approachable and friendly. We became friends with many of them over time.

One particular neighbor turned out to be one of the friendliest and one of the most interesting people to know. He was, by trade, a computer engineer, but he was much more than that. He always had at least two motorcycles in his garage at any given time. He would ride one while the other was being rebuilt. His garage was always spotlessly clean and organized. That never made any sense that he was so organized because he always had a project in the works outside of his bike rebuilds. If he saw me out in my yard, he would yell at me to come over to see his latest project. That was one of the highlights of my day.

I loved hanging out with him. There would always be a jovial discussion about anything that entered our heads.

He was inventive and daring. I was always around for an introduction to the latest big-deal project of the year, and he was never disappointing. One year, he and his older son decided to each build a motorcycle out of a lawn mower. Within a couple of days, my new friend had his up and running. It was a trike with the gearshift between the legs. All the neighbors came outside, watching as he started popping wheelies in the street. We all laughed and applauded. It was as if we were all part of his pit crew as he rode past all of us on the street in a celebratory fashion.

Over the years, there were neighbors that came and left. My friend was one of them that left. But so did other great neighbors. There was Steve and Annett, Terry and Emily, Mica and Jake, Clair and Jan, Betty and Nels, and so many more. We stayed. It just didn't seem right to leave this neighborhood. Sometimes I feel like the neighborhood watchman. I like to see new people moving in and letting them know that it's going to be okay. There are too many other things to worry about. Your new neighbors should not be one of them.

I received a call from my friend's wife one day. She gave me some very disturbing news that her husband was suffering from a serious bout with cancer. He would not make it to Christmas this year. She asked if I would please give the eulogy for his service. Of course I said yes. There comes a time in all of our lives when we have to say goodbye. It is not easy, and the timing can be a challenge. Selfishly, this gave me the opportunity to give my friend a gentleman's send-off. As his friend, I knew a lot about him, and that helped to put together a respectable eulogy. But I still took the time to sit with his wife and talk about this man and his journey through this thing called life. Of course, there were events and fondness that I did not know about. This helped to cross some t's and dot some i's.

When the day came to eulogize my friend, the chapel was filled with loved ones. It was pleasing to hear stories of him from coworkers and other friends. As I began the service, I asked that we all bow our heads in prayer. Now, my friend was not a religious guy and probably would not care one way or the other if we had skipped that prayer; but as I listened to some of his mourners earlier, it was clear that many in attendance would like to say a prayer for their friend.

As I chronicled his journey through life and witnessed the faces of his gathering, it became clear to me that all of our lives are a witness to other lives.

Let us be faithful to the gathering of truth in our lives. Let us remember the light in the eyes of our fellow human beings as we speak of life. Allow the breath of adventure to seep into our world. Let no one stifle the sound of our journey, and we will be remembered as we are, true believers of the spirit within us.

I remember attending a peace rally along the Mississippi riverfront in Rock Island, Illinois, during the summer of 1968. The gathering got larger as the evening fell. We were kind to each other and would mingle. I talked with a fellow from Chicago that day and asked why he made this trip. He told me that he had just lost his brother to enemy gunfire in Vietnam, and his parents were in such distress that he needed to be part of this event. He went on to describe how empty his life seems without his best friend and brother and how lost he and his parents are. I think that was the moment that I realized none of us should feel that we are less than anyone else. It is wise to remember that you are important to someone.

The avenue of thought during these rallies were simply that human life is not to be discarded as an object to use for the sake of senseless war or, for that matter, anything other than forming a temple of love and respect for each other. Oh, it was a great time to be alive if you were privy to that way of thinking.

We were products of our education. In those days we were subjected to a different kind of education. Civics class was mandatory in order to graduate. We were subjected to critical thinking regarding politics and the need for understanding the branches of government. Some of us were so into this class that we also took up debate classes and formed debate teams. We learned how to subjectively and objectively respond to opposing ideas and feedback. It was a time when our parents were busy trying to make sense of the world right along with us. Our fathers were veterans of war, and our mothers took up the art of making a home for us all. They became saddled with a sense of confusion. As students of a different era, our parents knew that sometimes war is necessary in order to protect the good people of the earth. But the Vietnam War was a different animal. They were watching their children go off to a jungle of a war that had no path to victory. The United States was sent to help protect South Vietnamese against the Communist North Vietnam. Although that conflict was not our war at first, it became ours as we started losing troops left and right. Today, I still mourn the death of friends that came back in boxes. So our parents watched as our government was taking some of their children through a draft system and leaving some at home to protest that movement. I will be the first to admit that I wish we could have protested harder. Then maybe my friends and some of yours would be with us today.

There's a lot of debate today regarding education. Public education versus private schools are becoming a household talking point. It's important to teach your children that there are different views regarding this and what they are. Let them in on the debate. After all, it involves their education. Don't assume that they are not smart enough to be part of the discussion. You would be surprised by how well equipped they are with knowledge.

So peace rallies were a norm back in the sixties, as were Friday nights on the one-ways and crowded drive-in theaters. If you stayed home on a Friday night, it was usually because you were grounded. And then there were those who formed bands and spent most of their time in someone's garage annoying the neighborhood with loud drums and poor guitar playing.

I loved playing guitar and hung out with a few that did the same. We became a cult of sorts as band members would switch from band to band every now and then. There were some great bands in the area at the time. Unfortunately, I was never in any of those. It made no difference to me because I respected the one that was noted as superior to most. I was in awe of their dedication to excellence and would look for ways to improve myself just by watching them. My older brother, Tom, was the lead singer in one of those bands. I loved listening to these guys. I was never jealous, but I was a little envious of the talented guitar player Dave. As years moved on and we became adults, I lost touch with all of them except brother Tom. I started making new friends and doing other things like hunting and fishing and, of course, drinking.

There was no better "sport" for me than underage drinking. The thrill of getting away with purchasing alcohol and downing copious quantities of that sweet nectar, king alcohol. My favorite was beer. Any beer. I didn't care if it was brewed from the skin of dead monkeys. If it fermented into alcohol, then I was satisfied. It gave me the courage that I wanted and thought I needed to express myself freely. It allowed me to enter into adulthood with the knowledge that if I needed to numb the pain of growing up, all I needed was a twelve-pack and buddy to hang with. I hung with Gary, Fritz, and Steve and another Gary, Mike, Kenny, Dennis, Curt, Mel, and some guy from Bluegrass, Iowa, whose name I could never remember.

We drank and we fought. Sometimes we ate first, and sometimes we were very careful not to waste too much money on food.

The time got away from me. My grades were suffering, but I wasn't getting too much repercussions from home. My mother's health was failing, and she never let that known until it was too late. Dad always let Mom deal with us kids and our grades. I was starting to recognize my demise and started hitting the books to bring my scores back up. There was something inside me telling me to do this for Mom. I needed her to know that I was not a loser. How self-centered can one get? To think that my success was to power up the legacy of my mother, that her purpose in life could only be measured in how successful I was.

It was 1970, and I was a junior in high school. I was pleased with my first-semester scholastic achievements to this point. Walking home from school on a cold January afternoon, I was summoned by brother Tom to get in his car. I did, and as he drove off, he told me that we are going to pick up our sister and head straight to the hospital. Mom was not doing well, and Dad was there and one of my older brothers, John, and his wife Barb. My oldest brother, Jim, was serving in the navy overseas and was not present or even knew what was happening.

I was silent the whole trip. I was scared and confused. When we reached the waiting room and saw my other brother with his wife sitting there in a complete breakdown mood, I thought we were too late. Just then, Dad entered and asked me to follow him. We entered Mom's room. She was hooked up to so many things and was so jaundiced that I could hardly recognize her. Dad grabbed my hand and said to Mom, "Speed (that was my mom's nickname), Terry's here," and then he put my hand in hers. She could not speak and was breathing quite heavily. I told her I love her and began to cry. My dad then escorted me out and then, well, right there in the hallway of the ICU at Mercy Hospital in Davenport, Iowa, I realized that my life will be forever changed. I was not ready for this kind of change. I was sad, angry, frightened, and in complete destress. I wanted to run, but there was nowhere to run. I wanted to hide, but there was nowhere to hide. I didn't care about anyone or anything.

I just told my mother that I loved her, and I was certain that she did not understand. I knew that she would die without knowing how much I loved her. She was all I wanted at that moment. Everyone else could just go to hell as far as I cared. The world just stopped spinning for me, and for the first time in my life, I knew that it wasn't me that made her who she was. It was her. This sweet lady from Denison,

Iowa, who grew up in Davenport, fell in love with my dad, had five kids, was the oldest of three girls, born in 1919, who gave her adult life to raising five kids, was about to take her last breath.

I stood there in shock. I could feel her spirit as she drifted above me. All of a sudden, right after my sister left her room, my dad entered with tears in his eyes and announced that Mom had passed. I could hear crying and condolences. I felt a tap on my heart. I believe to this day that was Mom telling me that she loved me too.

We are not alone. I believe that we have a spirit within our souls that guides us to new heights. We just need to listen and follow its path.

Relinquishing the path to destruction is sometimes blurred by foreign elements, such as alcohol or drugs and even bad influences. I used my mother's death as a crutch to go back to the burrows of king alcohol.

My true friends would let me know that I was heading in the wrong direction while others would pal up to me at the bar as long as I was buying. There was no clear direction for me at this stage of my life. I felt like I was completely on my own. Reality was no longer an option. Although I had plenty of resources to rely on, such as family and even AA, I hardly needed any of them to help me feel sorry for myself. Booze and I could handle that all by ourselves.

Over the years, I would find help and then revert back to alcohol. I did this a time or two until finally, I had had enough. There's never a clear path to destruction. It takes time and a lot of twists and turns to get yourself into a world of calamity. When I finally reached the bottom of the bottle, I realized that this was not helping me or anyone else. My wife Mary had dropped some hints a time or two, but she was never so direct with me that I felt any fear of losing her. Later, I would discover that I wasn't tuned into her very well. Alcohol will do that to you.

It was March 14, 2009. I searched out the closest Alcoholics Anonymous meeting in Fullerton, California. It was a Saturday, and you have to know that this time, I had to be serious because Saturdays were always great drinking days. I remember sitting and discussing my demise with a fellow drunk, and he would laugh every now and then. I was getting concerned about his lack of compassion, but I continued and he invited me to attend meetings where he frequented.

There's no better feeling to a freshly sobered-up drunk than to walk into a place where you find out that you are not alone. It would be several meetings before I would understand why my new friend laughed when I was unloading on him with all of my worldly reasons for drinking and then stopping. It turns out that my story is just like his and so many others before me.

All the destruction that was littered behind my every move over the years would not just go away just because I quit drinking, but because I quit drinking. I could now find the strength and proper paths to right some wrongs. I began to understand the agony and pain that others are experiencing. The world was not focused on just me. There were people who depended on me, and I failed them. How fortunate am I to have another chance at life! Well, I'll know as I approach my final day on earth. But until then, I hope to be a positive element to the advancement of those who look to me for guidance of any kind.

As time has gone, I have had the ears of a lot of old drunks that have decided to change their lives for the better and save mine. Every day, I learn that I have to take this thing one day at a time. If you hang around the AA clubs long enough, you will hear those words like a salute or a greeting of sorts. I thank God every day for bringing me to that bottom when he did so I could meet some of the most powerful people I have ever known. When I walked into that place for the first time, they told me to sit down, listen, and keep an open mind. I sat, I listened, and all I had left was an open mind. I tried to control my drinking like a normal person, and all that got me was further into the bottle.

Now, I'm not going to preach about the evils of alcohol. No one likes a preachy old sober drunk. My reasons for bringing this out is to let you know where I came from and how I got sober. There were some pretty dark days way back then. When I think about the messes

I made and people I hurt, I can pretty much tell you that step 9 never ends. I am constantly in the rear on amends.

Perhaps there are moments in our lives that were turnstiles to another dimension. As long as we free our minds to listen and accept others as they are, then we will be a part of the lives that guide us through this thing called life. How fortunate we are that we can look for utopia in the places of the heart. I see this world as a place of free imagination. How wonderful it is that we can all believe in different gods to worship but still look across the table and see a beautiful soul. Remember to see your heart before you see the cross. Remember to listen to the spirit of the voice that sings and not the evil that tries to drown out the tone. So keep an open mind and bring your world with you and share it as you grasp the ideas of others. I spent many days believing that I was all alone. When I discovered that others were there with me, we became a team. We are free to ask for help and free to give as we may.

Remember that your last day is not the day to work toward. Today is that day.

CHAPTER 12

Rest Easy

Go up the mountain with the snow to the top
The ease of a life is not yours to stop
The breeze in the air might blow towards your breast
but it's not yours to stifle
let it travel to rest

Follow the rising of wills and of light
you're not going to leave here
there's nothing to slight

I'm with you I'm here
I'm open to there
so don't leave here wondering
who's here and who's there

So rest on the mountain
take it easy and smile
You're only here once   .
Rest Easy *with style.* (TK White)

Thanks to the ease of modern technology, I have been able to sustain enough energy to write about the ups and downs of the world in the death-care industry. I want you to know that I am of no authority on any one subject other than my own personal experiences throughout my years in different positions where I have had the pleasure of helping others. In the short amount of time that I worked as a funeral associate, I worked with real professionals. People have had to sit with grieving families and sometimes the angry uncle who refuses to believe that the cost to send his loved one off to another dimension is out of line with what he thinks it should cost. As noted in chapter 3, there are a lot of people and products that go into the making of a successful and respectable funeral. One of the costliest features to running a funeral home is insurance, liability and everything else that goes with owning any business. If you don't believe me, check with any reliable insurance professional. That cost is staggering and keeps going up year after year.

This is where you as a responsible adult come in. You do have control over the cost of yours and even your loved ones' funeral expenses. The term is *preneed*.

Earlier, I talked about getting to know your local funeral professionals. It is as easy as that. I encourage everyone to sit with a funeral professional and discuss your future needs. They will guide you through what is known as a "preneed" process. You will be given options regarding the cost of your funeral and all the products that go with it. As you age, you have the option to add to your preneed or even have it transferred to another funeral home in another town. In most cases, you can spread the cost out over a period of time so that you are not strapped to shelling out a bundle of cash right there on the spot.

When you think about the burden, it is for your loved ones to have to sit in front of a funeral director and try to put together a respectable funeral at today's cost when this could have been diverted if you had just been proactive.

There were times, during my years on the supply side, that I would get a call from a funeral home to send a truck and pick up a casket because the family didn't have the money to spend so they just had Mom cremated. Don't get me wrong, I believe that cremation is a respectable way to exit the earth, but as I put myself in the seats that were occupied by that grieving family, I could not help but wonder how defeated they must have felt. It was bad enough to lose Mom; now we can't even have the funeral that she would have wanted. The fact is that most people are unaware that they can work with a funeral home to have the celebration of their choice if they can find the time to sit with them and discuss arrangements. In many cases, the funeral professional will come to your home. How convenient is that?

The cost of goods and services will fluctuate over time. In most cases, they will rise. That is just the nature of doing business. Costs rise for various reasons. When I was shipping caskets, we were subjected to raw material cost increases as well as fuel and labor and a gazillion other things like insurance cost increasing, and that guy who cleans your office has to feed his family too. The upside to paying for your preneed funeral before that day actually comes is that you are able to control that cost.

Unless you are familiar with your local funeral home, you can search by going to nfda.org. At the top, click on "For Consumers." Follow the link, and they will lead you to a funeral home in your zip code.

Another option that you will discover while visiting with your newfound funeral friend will be your choice of celebrant. You can check with your church that you are a member of, or you can choose from a list of celebrants that the funeral home keeps on file. Either way, you will have someone there to send you off to the heavens.

I highly encourage you to stay close to your friends and family so that the decisions that you make are based on the love from others and not just a reflection of your own visual on your life.

If you think about a ten-year-old child, you will immediately be reminded of innocence. But by the age of ten, they have an entire decade of experience behind them. They learned to speak, walk, control their bladders, tie their shoes, take directions, and ignore everything you tell them. A ten-year-old is thinking about the freedom of their upcoming teen years. While they still believe that the opposite sex has cooties, they are beginning to wonder what makes them tick. They have yet to see your paycheck but believe that you are stinking rich. Your boy thinks that Timmy down the street has way cooler things to play with than he does. Your daughter thinks that Melanie down the street is a bitch. The mind of a ten-year-old is way past what you imagine it is. But they are a product of their environment. They learn to cope with life by watching how we handle things. They have feelings and get mad and hurt just like we do, but they are sometimes not sure how to express those feelings. You would think that ten years would be long enough to have them trained and on the road, but they keep making mistakes. We work with them and give them ideas on how to handle things. Now, all of this might seem funny, but you have to admit, I'm not far off. The reason I bring up our ten-year-olds is because it reminds me of myself through my life journeys.

I am also a product of others. My wife Mary has had a huge hand in molding my thoughts and my beliefs. There is no one that I know who could light the world on fire with their love like her. She has the heart of a goddess and the soul of a troubadour. Just being close to her fills me with hope. I just know everything is okay when I'm around her. My parents were more of the kind that trained you enough to get you rolling and then turn you loose. Don't get me wrong, they were both loving people and would be there for me if I needed them. With three older brothers, I was usually pawned off to one of them, so I developed some crazy ideas on how to cope with life. I am also graced with the brilliance of my daughter Sarah. I am not sure when I stopped being the teacher and started being the student, but as far back as I can remember, I am reminded to turn left when I want to turn right. When I go off on certain tangents and all reasoning leaves my soul, Sarah is there to put me back on track. She will ask me for advice from time to time, but that's usually about where to look for the remote. I am fortunate to have such a brilliant and wonderful daughter who has taken life by the horns and took charge. When I was down and out, she never beat me up. When I started climbing out of my hole, she was there for me in every way. There are spirits and then there are angels. She's both.

There are many more who have been there for me. You might be one of them. I watch and listen to those that will speak, like my older brother Jim. I have a platoon of people whom I trust and admire. If I named you all, I'd run out of paper.

As a supplier of funeral supplies, a funeral associate, and a celebrant, I have had countless encounters with grieving families and can honestly say that the hardest part of all this is when a family member can't let go. It is trying to express what it means to have lost a loved one, but for those who are not prepared for that loss, it is even worse. The suffering is unbearable for them. They can't imagine life without their loved one. They slip into such deep depressions that they dwindle into an unrecognizable being. Suicide is not out of the question, and life takes on no meaning at all.

If you know someone like this or if you are someone like this, please call *the suicide hotline*: 1-800-273-8255.

Suicide is nothing to fool around with. Let's make this perfectly clear: we all lose when someone takes their own life. Some believe that they are just putting themselves out of their own misery. The truth is that there are people around them who love them and feel to blame for their demise. And then it starts all over. Always remember that you are not alone. Ask for help.

I hope that everyone who reads this book comes away with an approach to life that makes you all happy. There are as many avenues to that plateau as there are human souls. Find a hobby, write a book, bring a new feeling of experience to your well-being. There are times when we all feel overwhelmed with life. Take time to relax and remember to bring it home. One of the problems with society today is that we tend to get comfortable in a corner that we put ourselves in and we just stop looking for a way out. As this coronavirus continues to spread, school districts are trying to come up with ideas in order to keep our children and teachers safe. As I listen to one district talk about one idea and another comes up with something completely different, I'm wondering if they even talk to each other. Where is it etched in stone that schooldays need to be Monday through Friday and from 7:00 a.m. to 3:00 p.m.? I can verify for a fact that parents work weekends and different hours of the day. A town hall meeting of sorts would be a step in the right direction. If they just allowed parents to have a say, there could be some great ideas out there. In other words, talk to each other and get some ideas on how you can handle your grief. How can you work through the pain? You can't if you don't talk and listen.

Anyway, this is a good time to find out what you are capable of. Look for ideas to spread your wings. Everyone has the capacity to turn left after you have been turning right this whole time.

Pictured here are a few items that I made during the 2020 COVID-19 quarantine.

Funerals are nothing to make light of, and I hope that I was able to put a new spin on the industry for you. Over the years, there have been heartaches and disappointments. But there was always a path through to the other side. I have a lot of people to thank for that.

If you know someone in the funeral industry, take some time to sit with them and let them walk you through a day in their life. It takes a special person to come to work every day and counsel the bereaved. It's never the same widow or sibling or granddaughter. It will always be a new face and a new story. There will be tears, and there will be sadness. The funeral director will greet each one with dignity and respect.

Rest easy.

Chapter 13

Losing a Child

There are moments in the death-care industry that will always pull at one's heart much harder than others. As a supplier, a funeral associate, a funeral director, or even a celebrant, the hardest part of this job are those days that include the death of a child.

As we prepare for our own last day, we are preparing our family and friends for the time that we will no longer be a part of the crowd. Although that day will be a sad day and a day to reflect on the good life that was a historical journey to our grave, it was usually expected and planned for.

There's no amount of planning or comforting that could be enough to relinquish the pain of losing a child. A mother reserves the scares and the heartbeat of their offspring in every case. They feel their pain, and they know how to comfort them. After all, these elements of love and innocence are part of Mom for nine months. It is difficult for any man to understand the level of oneness the mother feels during pregnancy.

So anyone could imagine the pain of losing a child at any age. Yes, the father and even siblings will feel that loss with enormous sadness as well. That is not for debate. There is a lot of love that goes around and is captured by all family members. We see our children as junior adults. We develop a subliminal vision of them growing up and becoming a huge part of our lives and society. We are proud as they grasp the knowledge of the spoken word and that first time they walk like a drunken sailor across the room. But sometimes we are robbed of those moments. Sometimes a mother will be forced to lose their baby through an ectopic pregnancy or miscarriage or stillbirth. There is no control that a mother can have against any of these. But they feel responsible and suffer a tremendous amount of depression and pain. While many mothers will ride through a bout with postpartum depression, many mothers will experience this for a limited time. While we understand that postpartum depression is a chemical imbalance that is triggered through the experience of giving birth, it does, however, create quite a mind-blowing experience for Mom. For nine months, she has had a closeness that becomes a part of her life. She feels every kick and movement. She eats for two and carries her lifeblood around everywhere she goes. There is no amount of worldness that can compare. Now couple postpartum with the loss of a child through ectopic, miscarriage, or stillbirth. There is no amount of comfort for that loss.

There are also the families that lose their little ones after months or even years postbirthday. That doesn't make the loss any less devastating.

As a supplier, I kept child's caskets toward the back of the warehouse. I didn't like to see these on a regular basis. When we had an order for one of these small caskets, I would have my own moment of silence and bow my head. These always represented the tears that are falling for a life that never got the chance to explore all that life has to offer. I always imagined a mother in complete distress and a family that now has a void so big that no one can fill.

Fortunately, we didn't see these very often, but they would appear, and we would reflect on what could be.

There are also parents who lose their child through other avenues, including drug and alcohol abuse, violence, and even accidental death. These are no less devastating. A child is a child is a child. They do not graduate out of childhood just because they grew up. Mary and I still worry about our child who has grown to be a very successful member of society. It never stops. The love of a child is a phenomenon that can only be explained through the experience of having them. Keep in mind that a mother's loss through ectopic, miscarriage, or stillbirth are still mothers and suffers as the mother of a teen or adult.

As we are all aware that the cost to send our loved ones off to the heavens can be a struggle if you haven't prepared for that day, it is even more so for the family of a lost child. Below is a list of organizations that can be helpful for those who need assistance. I understand how devastating it is to lose a member of the family. It is more so to lose a child. You will never be prepared for this trauma. Of course, no one would be expected to be. There are organizations that will step up and help with cost, mental health, burial needs, and everything that goes with that. You can also count on your local funeral directors and let them guide you through this heart-wrenching process. Below in an organization that is dedicated to the needs of a family who has lost a child.

You can contact: http://littlelovefoundation.blogspot.com/.

I hope that you will never have to make this connection, but if you do, they are a wonderful organization. Please pass their information to those who are in need.

Keep in mind that Little Love Foundation is not a financial organization, but they do have a list of organizations that do offer assistance.

When we lose a child, we think that there is no amount of worldly deeds that will comfort your heart. It is normal to digress into a dark world and keep everyone out. The people and things that were important to you for years have taken a backseat to your pain. Nothing makes sense, and you feel obligated to no one and nothing.

It is important that you seek help and to let someone take that journey with you. There is help for you. Your funeral professional can suggest the right avenue. Remember that they have been helping families in distress for years. There will be professionals to help with parents of a child lost to suicide and for those who lost a child to cancer or any avenue that needs to be addressed. I hope this helps.

CHAPTER 14

Final Thoughts

Over the years, I have had the honor of knowing some great people who have dedicated their lives to serving others. I could go through a list as long as my arm, but the point is that we all have a sense of wanting others to be safe. No one wants to see another one suffer no matter what the circumstances are. This book was an idea that I have had for a few years now. I wanted to let everyone know that there are people who are there to help along the way in this jungle that we call life.

Time has prepared me for despair and, of course, the gift of love. It has brought me to a sense of understanding of circumstances. I can no longer wish anyone ill will. I understand that we all have families and responsibilities.

In the years to come, there will be heartache. There will be loved ones moving on to the heavens. You may be one of them. Move toward that day with all the gusto you can. Take that trip. Try that dish. Go to that concert. Do the things that you know you will be disappointed if you didn't.

You will be met with times of sorrow and sadness. I hope that I have proposed ideas that will guide you through those times. In this world, there are a number of lives that have dedicated their days to helping those in distress over the loss of a loved one. Prepare yourself with the knowledge that you are never alone. Follow your heart, but never be afraid to share the path you are on. I mentioned that the human race is a strange species, and I think you will agree. There are those that we want to be around and those that we would rather close the door on. Don't let your path be crowded with the latter.

From time to time, you will have moments when you want that path cleared, and that is okay. Just don't forget the ones that kept you company when you needed it most.

Now, enjoy each day that's left and remember:

Rest easy.

CPSIA information can be obtained
at www.ICGtesting.com
Printed in the USA
LVHW090500050521
686547LV00001B/19

9 781637 901229